Catholic Lives I

Dolores Julie Foti-Grant

Via Dolorosa

Father James Grant

Modotti Press

"where religion does matter"

Copyright © 2023, James Grant

Catholic Lives Series, 2023.

ALL RIGHTS RESERVED. This book contains material protected under International and Federal Copyright Laws and Treaties. Any unauthorised reprint or use of this material is prohibited. No part of this book may be reproduced or transmitted in any form or by any means, electronic or mechanical, including photocopying, recording, or by any information storage and retrieval system without express written permission from the publisher.

Modotti Press, an imprint of Connor Court Publishing.

CONNOR COURT PUBLISHING PTY LTD
PO Box 7257

sales@connorcourt.com
www.connorcourt.com

Front cover picture by Brad Ashlock

ISBN: 9781922815316

Cover design by Ian James

Printed in Australia

In grateful rememberance of Nicola and Fortunata Foti, parents of Dolores, Maria and Larry; and Monica Spencer, teacher of Dolores

Dolores Julie Foti-Grant

Born 16 February 1956

Entered into eternal life 15 May 2022

PREFACE

"Love your life while you have it. Life is a splendid gift. There is nothing small in it. For the greatest things grow by God's Law out of the smallest. But to live your life, you must discipline it. You must not fritter it away in 'fair purpose, erring acts, inconsistent will' but you must make your thoughts, your words, your acts, all work to the same end, and that end not self but God." (Florence Nightingale)

To the people who had the courage to begin without any guarantee of success: Jeanne-Marie Cilento, Pravin Rodrigues, Adriana Verdini, Paul McDonnell, Dolores Grant, Tim Lynch, David Abbott (Save St James Brighton commitee).

For the love between siblings – Dolores, Maria and Larry and for the gift of friendship – Lynne McKay, Anna and Neil winter, livia Vecranges.

CONTENTS

1.	A Modest Person of Extraordinary Depth	9
2.	Gratitude	11
3.	Remembering	13
4.	Humility	15
5.	Principles Matter	19
6.	Loyalty	21
7.	Cultivate Excellence	23
8.	Forgiveness	31
9.	True Feminity, True Manhood	37
10.	The Fighter	41
11.	Freedom and Responsibility	47
12.	Freedom, Free Speech and Australia's Future	51
13.	Dead End Thinking	59
14.	Courage	65
15.	Suffering	71
16.	Culture	75
17.	The Beauty of Tradition	79
18.	Prayer – Small Steps, Lasting Impact	87
19.	Why Go to Mass?	93
20.	What God is Like – A Dolores View	97
21.	The Communion of Saints: Praying to and with Dolores	107
22.	Catholicism: The Family Faith	111
23.	Dolores – our Family Saint	115
24.	Via Dolorosa – Look After My James	117
25.	Miraculum Dolores	121
26.	The Love of Dolores for Mary	129
27.	How To Pray the Rosary	133

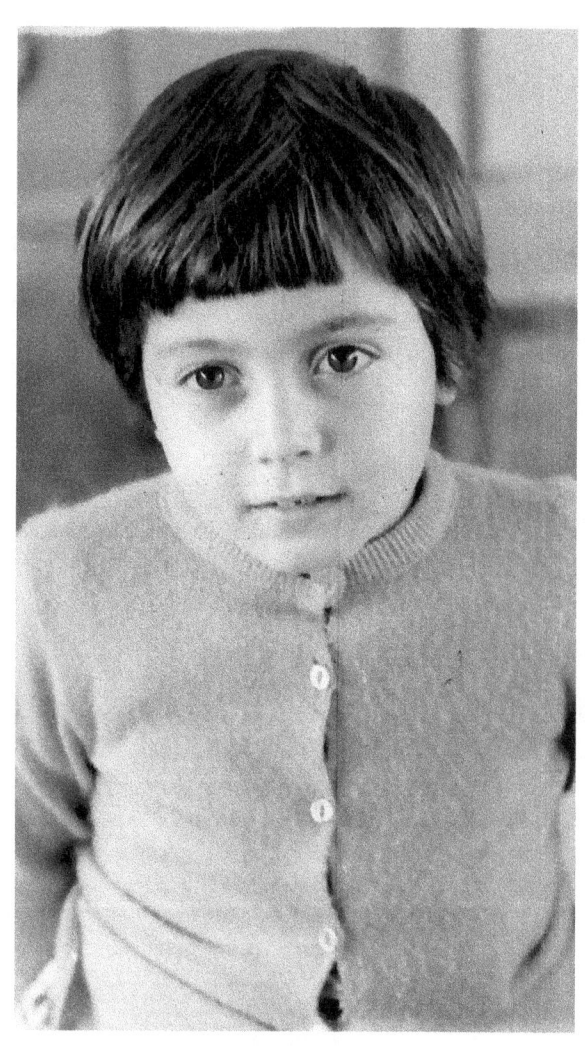

Doroles, circa 1960.

1
A Modest Person of Extraordinary Depth

Dolores Julie Foti-Grant was a very modest person but there was a lot happening beneath the surface that you would only see and understand if you spoke to her. At the time of her death on 15 May 2022 Dolores had profoundly affected the lives of thousands of people and, most importantly, an encounter with Dolores was a life changing event.

We hear stories of wonderful people who do good things every day, yet few of us are able to change lives in the manner that Dolores did, not just with adaptations but complete transformations of broken, hostile, and angry lives turned onto new paths of reconciliation, contentment and renewed purpose.

All this begs a major question – how on earth did she do this? Was there a hidden secret? How did such a small, quiet and humble person impact the lives of so many – to the point where

I have never met a person who did not comment on the amazing impact of meeting Dolores. Many people have suggested to me that Dolores was a naturally good person, a person who was just 'born good'. That is not the case – Dolores made choices each day to be a better person, to try a little harder, to start again, to forgive and ask others how she could go about making a particular situation better. She asked me those questions every day, but I am not the person who she asked most often, at any time, day or night. That privilege belongs to the Blessed Virgin Mary, mother of Jesus, most particularly in her expression of Our Lady of Lourdes.

The practical life of Dolores was energized and sustained by something beyond herself; a devotion to Mary, yet she brought some particular and practical aspects to this relationship. That combination of devotion to Mary and her own unique view of the world offers us a way of living worth considering. This small work offers perhaps a few tiny steps to help each of us journey on a path to a better life, yet on another level is a profound path to a life of eternal fullness. In the case of Dolores Foti-Grant, no-one who knew her is of any doubt of its power and its workability.

2

Gratitude

In modern Australia we live in a fundamentally self-orientated society. 'My needs, my wishes, my expectations' are often at the top of our concerns. It is easy to see Government, workplace, service providers, and associations as being designed to serve me. Yet, for Dolores the primary 'service' arrangement was in another direction. The honour, thanks and gratefulness owed to her parents were the first and fundamental plank. This is not to suggest that her parents were perfect or always right, but she valued their viewpoint, sought their friendship and always looked to help and support them. She spoke to them every day by phone. The closeness of the relationship did not always guarantee harmony but it did ensure that the ability to communicate openly and put up with her dad's "appalling" jokes could be the basis of a relationship.

Dolores knew instinctively that to diminish your love and respect for your parents would result in individuals who were unhappy, self-hating and with ongoing grudges against the world. Her parents were not perfect but she was constantly grateful to them for teaching her about life and giving her encouragement in her first steps. Not one day elapsed without a short prayer to Mary for the gift of her parents – a simple and beautiful idea forgotten by many of us. If we forget to say 'thank you' to the people who nurtured us into the world can we really expect to be people who are able to 'love' anything else? Gratitude to parents is as simple and life giving as a two minute call or prayer per day.

3

Remembering

Dolores had a beautiful habit of remembering birthdays, weddings, favourite places and foods, children's names, pets and significant events in so called 'ordinary life'. In my view, the act of remembering such basic information offered the potential for a profound connection. How many of your friends ring you on your birthdays or anniversaries? How many know the stories of when you first met or what your feelings are in certain places? Of course, Dolores didn't remember any of these things – she bothered to write them down and then chose to make time to call you and celebrate special moments. She thought specifically about little gifts to buy you or mementos you might like. She spent hours over particular cards or flowers just chosen for you.

She honoured her family and friends by treasuring her friendships and then she drew closer by not only remembering but thinking about what she would say in a simple phone call or a short message. All these things are representative of self-forgetting and putting others first. Some might say such actions and behaviours are not really much, so simple that anyone would do them.

Yes, but we don't, we don't place others above ourselves in such a way. For Dolores, love, respect and friendship are not measured by what we might do, but by what actually costs us time, even just a few short minutes. Dolores prayed for all her friends, relatives and complete strangers at these times. Not because she thought you might be in trouble, or lonely or downcast but because she wanted to 'celebrate' you before God, because she wanted to thank God for you, for your goodness, for your uniqueness. For Dolores none of this effort was wasted; on the contrary to talk to 'Our Lady' about your wonders, personality and beauty was never seen as a silly thing but was at the heart of who you are. Dolores just gave thanks to God for the gift you brought to this world. In almost every case prayer did not amount to complexities or hurdles to be overcome, it was just a grateful thank you.

4

Humility

Perhaps the central characteristic of Dolores' life was one of humility. When I watched people 'talk' to Dolores I was often aware that something had changed. Many people would comment to me after a discussion with Dolores that this was an "unusual" experience, normally people would simply say "I was really listened to" or "She seemed to know me after a few short minutes" or "It felt like we had known each other all our lives".

Whilst I was aware of this 'change', it was never discussed between us, thought about or considered by her as a 'religious thing'. I talk to myself often about being more humble, more considerate, more thoughtful of others. Dolores never talked about such things yet to meet her was to experience a depth in her life that overwhelmed with understatement, consideration and attention to the needs, hopes and dreams of others. For Dolores, humility was not a skill you acquire. It was something you do and it did not seem to require thinking or planning.

Humility for Dolores was not a thing that you 'switched on'. It was never a one-off event or a single conscious instance; it was just how she related to others. Yet there was a series of profound ideas wrapped up in her general approach to meeting and talking to others. Primarily, she seemed unconsciously to be asking herself 'What do others need?' Her focus was never on her stories, opinions or ideas. She seemed to concentrate on 'your' story and could quickly identify those things that troubled you, that you hoped for and her response after 'long listening' was always about solutions to what you had said. Dolores was always keen to 'meet you'.

Dolores intrinsically linked devotion to life, devotion to others and devotion to God, to a form of listening which was the essence of life. It was not just God or Our Lady who needed her devotion, but people also needed her devotion. They needed her prayers, her affection, her patience, her suggestions, her total attention. Dolores was devoted to people in a profound way that underscored her respect for others, her recognition of your importance and as a 'method' for seeing others. For Dolores if you are not devoted to people (not just your friends) then as a person what could you really be on about? How could we claim to love God and Mary, if we did not respect with humility and honour, the gifts that God himself has made? Her devotion to others was a sign of her recognition of the centrality of you, in the scheme of God.

Perhaps the best example of this is again found in Our Lady and her "yes" to God. This was not an example of self-exultation, but a recognition of the centrality of God's plan for each of us. When Dolores listened or spoke to others she fundamentally acknowledged and noticed God's plan for you and she got out of the way, seeing the essential action as the 'calling' of God in your life. It was no wonder or surprise to me that people in this experience saw something happening that was beyond themselves or beyond the experience of meeting Dolores; perhaps that is the real definition of humility that Dolores understood – by allowing herself to be devoted to others, she allowed new and exciting prospects to happen.

> "In the sixth month the Angel Gabriel was sent from God to a city of Galilee named Nazareth to a virgin betrothed to a man named Joseph and the Virgin's name was Mary. And he came to her and said "Hail, full of grace, the Lord is with you!" And the Angel said to her "Do not be afraid, Mary, for you have found favour with God and you will conceive and bear a Son, and you shall name him Jesus. He will be great and will be called the Son of the most high and the Lord God will give him the throne of his father, and of his Kingdom there will be no end". And Mary said "Behold I am the servant of the Lord, let it be done to me according to your word."" (Luke I, 26-38)

Mary said 'yes' to God without knowing what will happen and how it all will end. In a similar way the 'yes' of Dolores was not contingent on understanding or knowing of God's plans, but only on understanding and knowing you.

5

Principles Matter

Dolores was sometimes described by those who did not know her well as "old fashioned" or "traditional" in her values and beliefs. This is a significant misreading of who she was. Dolores was actually highly principled and had developed and adhered to some fundamental ideas and unchanging beliefs. At the core of Dolores' spirit was an unchanging bedrock of principles which could never be compromised.

Dolores was often saddened to see her friends or work colleagues setting aside their principles, to get by or gain some form of short term advantage. The modern Australian habit of 'practical change to changing circumstances' was never a possibility for her because in the end she noticed that it does not lead to success or happiness. For Dolores, 'adapting' your principles was a sure sign that the 'spirit' of the individual was being hurt and damaged. Dolores took her beliefs and principles seriously, was never flippant about them, never made excuses for them. I never witnessed a single occasion where she compromised or adapted them. The strength of these quietly spoken principles was fundamental to who she was and I know strongly influenced others to consider her as a profoundly loving and substantive person.

6

Loyalty

Dolores was intensely and unwaveringly loyal to her friends, family, workplaces and her husband, but first both individuals and workplaces had to 'prove' that trust with honesty and integrity. Her loyalty was not given with ease. Dolores had a significant ability to judge those she could rely upon, and those who were capable of showing these values, even if she did not always witness them every time in every person. Her loyalty was often coupled with significant forgiveness and encouragement. Certainly, sometimes people could disappoint and hurt her but she was never a person to write others off for human failings. It was always the general orientation of the person that she related with and that she sought to encourage.

The expression of her loyalty was always found in regular and ongoing contact and in taking it upon herself to engage with the lives of others, their sadness, their joy, their struggles. With Dolores you always received hands on practical help, not only words but actions. She would be the one to visit you in hospital, to help a parent or friend of yours, to buy you something you needed. The 'physical idea' of standing beside you was paramount. Loyalty did not qualify as two phone calls per year. Dolores was there for others, and that expression was month by month, year by year. Once you became part of Dolores' life you were never forgotten, or allowed to slip away with phrases that suggested we are all too busy or the pace of life prohibited contact

Dolores was also capable of having a say about the behaviours of others, especially if she thought you were letting yourself down. This was always in the most gentle and caring ways but it would still be pointed out. Perhaps a strong example of this centred on her belief and expression of marriage. Marriage was full commitment, companionship, friendship, caring in sickness, discussing problems. She had no truck with the idea that relationships can be stretched to include 'add-ons". She was always radically hurt and disappointed with the idea of "What happens in Sydney stays in Sydney!"

In our own life, the 'package' of marriage was so profound and Dolores and I were able to live this together. Dolores always saw her own marriage as an example of how it could be. She was immensely proud of her married life, as I was of her. There is much to recommend this approach as Dolores was so committed to her marriage that she lifted and sustained my views as well. Dolores definitely taught me about the beauty of 'full' commitment to another. Like everything in her life, her marriage was full of dedication to the other – gentle and considerate but without forgetfulness or casualness.

Wedding of Anna and Neil Winter, June 2000, Adelaide, SA.

7

Cultivate Excellence

Dolores would constantly amaze people with her commitment to excellence. This was seen most closely in her intensity to regular maintenance, repairs and cleaning. Anything broken or in need of replacement was immediately scheduled for repair. This went to every dimension in life – her car, her house, her personal possessions, her clothing, her garden, her health. Things needed to be maintained to high standards, yet this idea went much deeper than first observed and for Dolores ultimately indicated things to others about the kind of person you are.

Dolores was a person who noticed her surroundings in most areas of Australian life. She was never interested in buildings, houses, products or consumer goods that might be functional or inexpensive but designed not to last. In a society where material goods are so poorly made, Dolores would often comment on the wider effect on young Australians. Why would young Australians be interested in excellence when most things will be disregarded in a few short years?

Her strong view was that we as Australians were generally not maintaining standards of excellence which ultimately influenced the way we trusted and dealt with each other. If we were lazy or slack in our personal appearance or treated the things we own with disdain how could we be expected to trust our fellow humans in decent and long-term commitments?

Dolores often noted that Australians only visit cathedrals on their travels to Europe, or could be disrespectful or noisy in Christian churches, but would never do this in a mosque or Balinese temple. This was profoundly disappointing to Dolores because it meant clearly that many individuals had lost the ability to distinguish between the ordinary and the sacred. If everything is to be judged in ordinary or secular terms where does our sense of wonder or awe get cultivated? For Dolores, wonder and amazement prompted lots of questions. Why did people wish to construct such structures, what are they saying about life, and why did they put such veneration into even the smallest parts of their construction?

For Dolores these buildings were designed to lift the human spirit and soul towards God, towards a beauty and depth that we rarely see in this life. Yet, they also told Dolores something about humanity – we are creatures designed to replicate the skills and beauty found in creation, and we reach our greatest fulfilment when we strive to live lives of beauty and excellence.

Dolores could be frustrated by a number of things in the Catholic Church – unintelligible sermons, lifeless liturgy and poorly maintained buildings – but perhaps her greatest irritation was in the construction of lifeless, cheap and ugly churches that fail to speak of the beauty and excellence of God. Yes, you can worship God in a tin shed, but that, for Dolores, is not what humans are called to be. For her, Catholics were called to be people of excellence and beauty, of something beyond ourselves, something that speaks to our love of God, but also of our care, concern and love for others.

Dolores was also often disappointed in our secular buildings: cheap, ugly and looking tired after only two or three years. Many of our trains, trams and buses are old, dirty and do not run on time. We live in a world where the demand for services is often unfulfilled, where maintenance providers are hard to find and where those who do not manage to be available are overworked and provide only temporary fixes. Short term functionality and inexpensive outcomes seem to have infected the thinking and expectations of those who provide much needed services into our lives.

Yet, for Dolores, this lack of excellence and attention to detail is also seen in our personal lives. For Dolores, excellence comes from within. If you cannot perform at your best, even when no one is watching, then how can you convince others that 'value' is part of who you are? If your home or personal space is dirty, messy and unclean then how can you convince others that your work performance will be of a high standard? For Dolores, it was the driving of excellence in difficult moments that drove excellence in the easier parts. Dolores could be extremely suspicious of those who put off completing relatively simple tasks. For her, they would invariably be found missing when the going became hard.

Finally, for Dolores, excellence was driven by an inner trait that most people overlook. When you say yes you will do something, do what you say. Excellence is found in completing tasks efficiently and without fuss. When you are able to complete tasks well and in a timely manner, you indicate to others that you are a trustworthy person and that your words and speech mean something. Indeed, for Dolores it went much further – you are a person who values and lives by excellence and personal honour.

> "He who is faithful in little will be faithful in much." (Jesus Christ)

> "The quality of a person's life is in direct proportion to their commitment to excellence." (Vince Lombardi)

James and Dolores wedding, Feb 2006, Melbourne, Victoria.

8

Forgiveness

Dolores commenced her working life in the late 1970s and early 1980s. This was not an easy time for young female office workers, especially those who worked in companies with established male bosses and a culture of work hard, make money and then party hard. Many of the long time senior managers often saw this environment as one where men could approach women for sexual favours, not only outside of work hours but also within the confines of the office environment.

Dolores suffered a great deal in the office environment through constant sexual harassment and innuendo. It was also the case that Dolores knew the wives, children and girlfriends of these men. Whilst she always refused to be involved in these activities she was deeply hurt for the girls who did succumb, for the wives betrayed and ironically even for the male perpetrators themselves.

In the 1980s there was no easy solution to such workplace problems. It was a balance of maintaining your private dignity, avoiding certain individuals and situations, trying to maintain work standards and relationships without getting fired or constantly looking for new opportunities. Dolores always encouraged other girls to maintain their personal dignity and not be seduced by flashy promises or short-term benefits. This was not an easy line to take and often raised tensions and suspicions from many different quarters.

Dolores took her standards and personal integrity from the actions and teachings of Jesus, particularly in her efforts not to judge the participants in these hurtful and often power-based interactions. She was astounded by the 'big picture' actions of Jesus towards the women caught in adultery.

> "The teachers of the law and Pharisees brought in a woman caught in adultery. They made her stand before a group and said to Jesus, "Teacher, this woman was caught in the act of adultery. In the law Moses commanded us to stone

such women. Now what do you say?" They were using this question as a trap, in order to have a basis for accusing him. But Jesus bent down and started to write on the ground with his finger. When they kept on questioning him, he straightened up and said to them, "Let any one of you who is without sin be the first to throw a stone at her". Again he stooped down and wrote on the ground. At this, those who had heard began to go away one at a time, the older ones first, until only Jesus was left, with the woman still standing there. Jesus straightened up and asked her "Woman, where are they, has no one condemned you?" "No one, sir", she said. "Then neither do I condemn you", Jesus declared, "Go now and leave your life of sin."(John 8, 1-11)

For Dolores, such office activities created no winners – everyone involved was degraded to positions that destroyed our humanity, potentially our families, but most centrally our souls and the very essence of who we were meant to be as individuals created by God. But none of this made it easier for her

– forgiveness on the surface did not appear to ease the daily tactics that she was subjected to and it confronted her in her efforts to be a person of dignity and ethics and yet not be broken and withered by such actions. This went on for many years, caused her many tears, and sometimes the feeling that that her prayers went unanswered.

In 2017, whilst Dolores was recovering in hospital from another surgical procedure, she was visited by a man who twenty years earlier had been one of her most assertive and obnoxious sexual predators. The man who stood before her was a broken and blubbering mess, a man who begged forgiveness for his long-term actions, but also recognized that his treatment of her and his attitude at that time had not only hurt her but destroyed his life, his family and his sense of humanity.

After many tears on both sides, Dolores saw the reaction and workings of God in releasing them both. This healing and forgiveness took 30 years to unfold. For Dolores, forgiveness was never cheap, pain lasted three decades and for her it was a constant work in progress that collaborated in the actions that God intended to undertake. Forgiveness is not easy or a switch to be turned on or off. For Dolores, it was a daily battle for many decades but the truth remains that without her constant emotional battle and daily prayer, the fullness of a human returned to rightful dignity could not have taken place. Now that is forgiveness on a whole other level.

Dolores circa 1977.

9

True Feminity, True Manhood

Dolores was utterly underwhelmed by the advent of aggressive feminism in both workplace and family life. This was not as opposition to women improving, developing or enhancing their personal or workplace lives but a reaction to the idea that men and women are competitors and that between men and women a state of mistrust, competition or victimhood could exist. For Dolores, the nature of men and women was found in the nature of what God himself had put in place and that reality saw a woman as the centerpiece of solutions to the world and individual problems.

> "My soul magnifies the Lord and my spirit rejoices in God my Saviour
>
> Because He has regarded the lowliness of His handmaid;

> For behold, henceforth all generations will call me blessed;
>
> because the almighty has done great things for me and holy is His name
>
> and His mercy is from generation to generation." (Luke I, 46-50)

In this statement of the historical Mary, Dolores found no mention of domination or competition between sexes, no mention of innate talents, no hint of inbuilt privilege; rather blessings and purpose come exclusively through the free gift of God and depend on only one thing: humility.

For Dolores, any individual male or female who sought to dominate, mock or control others was at risk of losing their humanity. Our humanity was to magnify the way God trusted us, our humanity was fundamentally co-operative, to mediate, to bring about solutions in the midst of hostility, pain and fear. That is what Dolores brought to all occasions of conflict and tension – not anger or hostility but a co-operative, partnering attitude, which did not come from weakness or fear but from a fundamental understanding of what humans were designed to be like.

In the mercy of Mary, Dolores found a way of being authentically human. It did not make any individual smarter or wiser but throughout her life Dolores found that by going to Our Lady to take refuge and protection in the 'mother of God' she was never disappointed; and so she took all of her problems, needs and worries to Our Lady, as she took the problems and worries of others as well. This humility, veneration and love was an imitation of Mary herself, who never let her down and allowed Dolores to see clearly that in spiritual terms battles between male and female are an utter irrelevance. The real battle is always within ourselves to be more humble, more attentive to God and therefore more authentic as people.

10

The Fighter

One of the strongest ideas embedded into our society and supported by most people is that 'failure is a bad thing'. Many of our insults are built around the idea that people who fail are somehow less worthy than others.

There is no doubt that the idea of failure and the fear of repeated failure is one of the reasons that many people give up their dreams of the future. There is also the distinct possibility that family members or your friends will be quick to tell you that you are not capable of achieving your goals or that you're not strong enough or talented enough to fulfil that future. 'Who do you think you are? Don't forget where you came from!' All of this is really code for 'We don't want you to succeed and we don't want you to do anything different to us'.

Dolores never thought in such a way, although her early school experiences contained a great deal of negative feedback, suggested she was a poor learner and would never amount to much. Perhaps these early experiences were the catalyst for developing her 'never give up' attitude. Her constant attitude was 'Try, try again and if you fail, go back and try again'. Perhaps her favourite family quote came from her father, Nicola, who constantly told her "Never let anyone put you down, even your family, and never accept that kind of treatment from anyone". This was certainly one of the greatest gifts from father to daughter!

Dolores was not made of different substance to you and me. She was not a superwoman, nor was she unaware of her failures. But she was able to keep going, to change course, to improve and to 'do life' differently. Why? What was the one thing that gave Dolores such resilience in the face of endless health issues and other disappointments? In my view, Dolores had subconsciously made an important connection: failure and action are intimately connected. This is a connection that is often not made because, overwhelmingly, when people fail they stop acting. For a majority of us, failure means stopping; when most people fall off a horse they do not get back on. The pain of failure, embarrassment, the fact that others note your failure – all contribute to most of us giving up.

For an individual like Dolores, failure meant more action, not less; failure meant questions about how things can be done differently and failure meant new ways of doing or approaching the tasks. What if failure could be seen as the necessary first step towards the onset of breakthroughs and success? What if we were no longer embarrassed by failure but stimulated by it as a path to greater success? This was always the attitude that Dolores took to failure and disappointment.

Last year I heard a great story of achievement. This story involved a young man with physical and psychological disabilities who took up martial arts. On his first lesson he could not manage a warm-up star jump, he could not master a forward roll, he could not speak to strangers and he could not understand basic instructions. Nevertheless, this man attended class faithfully for four nights a week, catching long bus trips to and from training.

For years and years his nightly experience was one of failure and starting again. No one in his school made it easy for him. In 2018, after 13 years of training, he finally achieved his black belt and made a heartfelt and intelligent acceptance speech in a public forum. Is this young man the best black belt in his school? No he is not. But is this one of the greatest achievements in Australian sport? Yes it is! Of course there are millions of better sports people whose skills and performance are widely admired. Given the starting point of this young man there are few greater individual achievements against adversity and failure. I doubt many of us would be able to persevere in this way, yet again in this story there is a strong connection between failure and renewed action.

This is how Dolores looked at the world of failure: it was never an excuse to give up. Dolores had many failures and she rarely achieved her goals after one attempt, yet she also knew that exposure to challenging events or circumstances made her mentally stronger. Small failures inoculated her against disappointment and was one of the factors that gave her such a positive and happy disposition. Dolores knew that she would get there in the end. Ultimately, it was not failure that made

Dolores a great and determined Australian but her response to those disappointments that made a successful life possible.

> "Failure is simply the opportunity to begin again, this time more intelligently." (Henry Ford)

> "Failure is not fatal, it is the courage to continue that counts." (Winston Churchill)

> "Our greatest weakness lies in giving up. The most certain way to success is always to try just one more time." (Thomas Edison)

11
Freedom and Responsibility

Dolores believed in the importance of your individuality and the uniqueness of your life. She saw your life as something exceptional and something that must be nurtured and inspired so that you can be the best person you could be and so that you also could make your 'yes' to God. For Dolores Australia was diminished if you are not able to make the best contribution that you can make, or if for some reason you had given up on such hopes.

For this reason, Dolores believed that you could never be defined by your racial or cultural background. She did not make assessments about you in relation to your religion, your family, your gender or your finances. She did not make judgements about you on the basis of where you live or the way you look. Dolores never judged you on any group identifications; she was only interested in your improvement and development as an individual. She believed your freedom, your individuality and your responsibilities were the greatest gifts you had been given.

Nevertheless, Dolores believed your freedom and your individuality must be fought for. That battle begins with yourself. Dolores was a gentle yet persistent challenger to all who did not strive to be their best, those who expected to receive something for nothing or those who thought the world owed them something because of background, family, race or gender. Dolores unashamedly believed in individual responsibility; she did not accept passivity, laziness or inactivity in relation to an individual's life and she was strongly anti those who would seek to control or downplay the freedom and rights of others. Your future depended on your willingness to try new things, to adopt suggestions and to put yourself forward to the best of your ability.

For Dolores, there were no 'great' people and the smallest or most insignificant did not get any kind of 'passes' from her not to participate, try their best or constantly seek to improve and make life easier for others. Her favourite religious stories always involved 'little people', not because they needed extra help or somehow enjoyed special privileges from God, but because it was they who made the greater difference.

> "Jesus sat down opposite the place where the offerings were put and watched the crowd putting their money into the temple treasury. Many rich people threw in large amounts. But a poor widow came and put in two very small copper coins worth only a few cents. Calling his disciples to him, Jesus said "Truly I tell you, this poor widow has put more into the treasury than all the others. They all gave out of their wealth; but she, out of her poverty, put in everything – all she had to live on." (Mark 12, 41-44)

Dolores listened to all kinds of excuses as to why something could not be done but she did not accept any of them – not shyness, not fear of public speaking, not statements that you have no skills or talent, or that your family did not love or accept you. Dolores had a persistent message – your life is important, take charge of it!

"As a human your greatness lies not in being able to remake the world but in being able to remake yourself." (Gandhi)

"There is nothing noble in being superior to your fellow man, true nobility is being superior to your former self." (Hemingway)

"He who conquers himself is the greatest warrior." (Confucius)

12
Freedom, Free Speech and Australia's Future

Dolores was immensely proud to be Australian. She viewed Western values founded on Catholicism, ideas of liberty, tolerance, economic freedom and the centrality of the individual as the fundamental path of giving everyone a fair go and creating a society that can benefit us all. In her own family, she witnessed the hard work of her migrant parents to get ahead and make a prosperous life.

Nevertheless, she was never naïve or blasé about Australian freedoms and the need to keep highlighting and fighting for their advancement. Dolores was a vigorous opponent of self-indulgent and interfering government regulations, especially in relation to political parties that tried to punish people from getting ahead. She hated red tape and any regulation that punished hard work. Dolores advanced her own life on the simple premise of being prepared to work hard which usually meant for her a second job and often a third. She was a great supporter of those who had a 'work ethic' and was always willing to help and encourage those beginning the journey of making a better life.

One strong consequence of this 'individual self-determination' would also be seen in her strong opposition to 'communist', 'Islamic' or 'dictatorship' regimes which sought to deter others from being their best. In short, any government, political system, or local council that sought to suppress individual freedoms or economic prosperity had a strong opponent in Dolores. Any local council that advocated for spending money on political 'projects' had a fierce opponent in Dolores, particularly if they failed to trim street trees, clean gutters, collect garbage on time or sweep streets. The responsibility of the 'citizen' was paramount for Dolores but heaven help any local government body that 'forgot' its charter of 'community service' on even the smallest of issues.

Dolores was a great believer in free speech and in later years became distressed at the standard of our Australian news and current affairs programs, the poor standard of political debate, and the repetitious promotion of one or two particular views. Dolores felt that the beauty of Australian society lay in people pursuing values that enhanced the individual and the family.

She was always suspicious of political parties or governments that claimed to have a monopoly on truth. For Dolores, it was important to hear from as many competing viewpoints as possible. Her inkling that all was not well in the political environment and therefore our wider society has been increasingly supported by the facts. In 2003, 41% of countries had a free press; by 2016 this had dropped to 31%. In terms of population, the numbers are even more dire; only 13% of the world's population of 7.4 billion people enjoyed free speech in 2016. (Freedom House, 'Freedom of the Press' 2017)

Dolores regularly used internet providers to source information in a wider framework than was usually available on commercial television, the ABC or streaming services. Dolores was certainly concerned with the rise of online distress caused to younger people, and always advocated for parents to take a greater hand in controlling the content their children accessed in online forums.

Nevertheless, whilst online expressions may sometimes lead to real life harm, she did not conclude that placing restrictions on free speech was an effective remedy. On the contrary Dolores believed that freedom of expression is associated with less rather than more extremism. "The preventative effect of free speech on anti-social and criminal behavior seems strong" ('The Future of free speech' April 2020). Dolores felt strongly that suppression of free speech invariably amplified and sent underground views that should be challenged in public forums.

For Dolores, this was one of the great oversights of the Catholic Church, a church which is silent on its own beliefs and does little to challenge views that denigrated or mocked Catholic teaching needs to be contested. If the church does not stand up for values that hold human life to be precious, that strengthen families, and highlight the great gift of married life, what is its wider purpose and how is it fulfilling its divine purpose of transforming human society? Dolores had great compassion for individuals that fell on hard times, got depressed, or did things that let themselves or their families down. She had no understanding of why the Catholic Church, charged with upholding and strengthening such values, would remain silent or appeared afraid to enter the fray.

For Dolores, in the sufferings of Christ and the burdens of his blessed mother, the path of the church was clearly laid. In her own life this was very familiar with the Via Dolorosa (the way of suffering) and the wider struggles of family, friends and the church, but she was always disappointed by Catholic silence on such troubles and its failure to provide practical and engaging support. In the young girl Mary who said 'yes' to God, things like fear, anxiety, and lack of endeavor were always cast out – so what exactly was the church afraid of?

For Dolores, the Via Dolorosa was the path we all must take. In her own individual case she had over 30 years of sickness, hardship and pain, yet this never caused her to concentrate on or worry about herself; indeed it encouraged her to journey more fully with others because she had some appreciation of what they were going through.

Naturally, for Dolores, experiencing the way of suffering, not allowing it to dominate life and then to overcome it in compassion for others was at the heart of the Catholic understanding of the world.

In the Sorrowful mysteries of the Rosary, Mary not only journeys to Calvary with Jesus, but partakes in his suffering as we are all called to do. In the same way that Mary journeyed with Jesus, Dolores journeyed with Mary. As Mary endured the Agony in the Garden, the scourging at the pillar, the crowning with thorns, the carrying of the cross and the Crucifixion, in like manner this was the spirituality of Dolores. She stayed and talked to people in agony. She visited and knew of those in intense pain, she knew of those who were unjustly accused of things, she was prepared to help carry the cross of others and she experienced the pain of crucifixion that never seemed to end.

In all of those sorrowful aspects of life, Dolores knew them from personal experience, could see them in others and never failed to share this lonely road with others. Of course, she had one other great insight and advantage to give to others … she also knew of the Glory to come. She not only believed in the resurrection but she had seen in the life of Mary this destiny for those she knew and loved. Not once was Dolores ever let down by God or did she doubt the truth of the promises of Christ and Blessed Mary.

For Dolores, Our Lady was always comfort of the afflicted, health of the sick, refuge of sinners, the Queen of peace and, perhaps most importantly, the singular vessel of Devotion. I have no doubt that Dolores and Our Lady were united in this vision of the way to help both individuals and the world. The actions of Dolores go beyond what is possible for a human to act upon. They point to a partnership with Christ and the Queen of all the saints.

13
Dead End Thinking

Human living guarantees at some stage in our lives we will be hurt by others. Dolores had this experience regularly in her life as we all do, yet she was both careful and intentional in ensuring that her hurts would not be passed onto other non-involved people and that she did not stereotype or lessen others in any way by what might have happened to her in the past.

Most of us will have been hurt during relationships, feeling that a former partner, friend or lover was dishonest or unfaithful towards us. All humans will have periods in life where friends or work colleagues let us down and are false hearted in their actions. These moments can cause us to often have thoughts and comments about others that perhaps we do not really mean but can quickly get established in our thinking, suggesting that our experience somehow reflects a truth about all 'types' of certain people.

Of course it is easy for a woman after a break up with a man to suggest that this is typical male behavior. "All men are bastards" is usually just a silly throw-away line, but for some people such thinking becomes embedded as a truth and as a narrative on which to guide all future relationships with men. A person who buys into such a shallow story about other types of people, commonly goes on to ensure a life of little trust becomes the norm in their future encounters with others. A pattern established on this shallow thinking can be hard to change. Once we begin to see this pattern applying to all people, it is usually possible to easily "create this truth" in our heads to back such assertions.

In the same way men who consider that all women cannot be trusted or have tendencies to gossip are applying a poorly thought-out logic to 50% of the population. Such thinking is unproductive on many levels or it blinds us to the very same characteristics in groups we think do not behave this way to ourselves. Individuals who think that gossip is a female characteristic have not listened to talk back radio, or a football show that incessantly talks about which players should be traded or delisted by various teams in future seasons.

Dolores was very aware that Jesus himself was a victim of this kind of thinking. She had a deep understanding of the rejection that was a constant phenomenon in the life and public ministry of Jesus. She was aware that Jesus was abandoned by his own disciples at the crucifixion and that there was great opposition from many individuals and groups at the radical nature of his message.

> "On the Sabbath he began to teach in the Synagogue and many who heard him were astounded, but others said 'Where did this man get all this? What is this wisdom that has been given to him? What deeds of power are being done by his hands? Is not this the carpenter the son of Mary?', and they took offence at him, and he was amazed at their unbelief ... Then he went out among the villages teaching ... and they cast out many demons, and anointed with oil many who were sick and cured them." (Mark 6, 1-12)

Dolores had a similar attitude to Jesus: negative thinking needed to be challenged for the sake of the individual who suffered from it, yet sometimes it was impossible to change. That future change she left up to God. Certainly she recognized that change was always possible; her role was to perhaps plant a tiny seed, but the ultimate change and effect on the individual were God's business. These would revolve around prayers to Our Lady.

For Dolores, dead-end thinking could be heard in many conversations, but it was most commonly packaged in discontented or annoyed formats. Being aware of our own irritated discussions can help safeguard our own thinking or at least help us acknowledge the lack of logic or clarity in many of our own ideas.

For Dolores, individuals who feel that they are owed something by a workplace or that a Government should be doing more to fix problems or that their race, background or culture gives them special insights are often sinking into dead-end thinking. This thinking always suggests that 'others', those outside of myself, are responsible for my disasters or lack of progress.

Dolores always felt very sad when people developed this stilted form of thinking, for she believed it inevitably caused problems and conflicts in personal and work life but more importantly blocked and prevented the personal maturity that people need to flourish in life. For Dolores, your personal views were your business but above all she believed your great calling was to understand what God wanted for you in life and as a bi-product for you to make a great contribution to society!

> "Parents can only give good advice or put you on the right path, but the final forming of a person's character lies in their own hands." (Anne Frank)

> "Attack the evil that is within yourself, rather than attacking the evil that is in others." (Confucius)

> "When others bewail the failure of Government, you must speak of self-reliance, of personal responsibility, of individual pride and integrity." (Margaret Thatcher)

> "To those to whom much is given, much is expected." (Jesus Christ)

> "There is an expiry date for blaming your parents, for steering you in the wrong direction, the moment you take the wheel responsibility lies with you." (J K Rowling)

14
Courage

In March 2015, St James Brighton was burnt to the ground in a fire that police treated as suspicious. The parish was a viable community of around 350 parishioners, with a heritage-listed building of immense historical importance and one of Melbourne's most popular venues for weddings. Yet, like many Australian parishes it had suffered at the hands of a nefarious pedophile priest for a period of thirteen years in the 1980s and early 1990s. Perhaps more shocking than a deliberately lit fire, was the comment of one particular local celebrity and the insipid response of the Melbourne Archdiocese.

Within two hours of the commencement of the fire, which took five hours to control, the Australian actress Rachel Griffiths had gone on Melbourne ABC Radio to say, "I was quite elated when I heard the news this morning. It's always been a difficult building for us to drive past, because there has been so much tragedy and complicated feelings. We've attended many funerals of boys we know abused by that priest ... at the actual church that it occurred in".

To these supercharged and factually-distorted emotional comments, the Melbourne Archdiocese had no response. For those of us gathered that evening, including Dolores in tears to view her destroyed church still smoldering, the lack of a bishop to witness and console the parish family was noted and not inconsiderably added to the beginning of an awareness, "Why is nobody from the Church here? It feels like we are abandoned".

As events unfolded, it would indeed be the case that this parish was abandoned. The indifference to the needs of these parishioners quickly transformed into a Diocesan theological viewpoint that the Church should not be rebuilt in deference to the pain of abuse victims. This was despite the fact that the abuse by this priest was already twenty years past and had not occurred within the Church. This is not an excuse for injustice but it does highlight an Australian Catholicism in fear, who can no longer talk of death and resurrection and whose 'do nothing' attitude is a key factor in Australian Catholic decline.

The behavior of this former priest, deeply depraved and corrupt, was quickly commandeered to portray the Church as old, irrelevant, out of touch and part of something the new priest charged with ensuring closure referred to as "old Catholicism" which must never be revisited.

The fact that St James was the only church in the region with a significant devotion to Our Lady meant it was not seen as worthy of retention. In the following weeks a small group of parishioners formed the 'Save & Restore St James Committee'. Dolores was heavily involved in the first years of the group's long fight to see St James rebuilt. This was a small group of courageous parishioners, who were vilified, unsupported, laughed at, abused at public meetings and, in the case of Dolores, told by the priest that she was an irrelevant, stupid and superstitious woman for her devotion to Mary.

Instead of being turned into a multi-use

Modernist shell with a peripatetic altar with flashing lights and an enormous chicken-wire cross on the roof, as one of the parish priests wanted, the Save & Restore St James Committee have ensured that the church has had its interior and original tuck-pointed stone exterior and bell tower completely returned to its former beauty.

There was a long and protracted battle to make sure the interior was also restored solely as a church with all of its gorgeous mosaics, stained glass windows and soaring beamed ceiling. For more than five years, the committee questioned and put pressure on all of those in the Archdiocese who wanted to destroy St James "it would be better razed to the ground" or turn it into an ugly space that could even be used for "bingo and drinks" as the parish priest in charge, said at the time.

Dolores and the other members of this group understood that there must be courage before action can take place, and on a deeper level they understood that if there is no courage there can be no Catholicism.

This is the courage of the Virgin Mary who says her "yes" to God; this is the courage of

Jesus in his encounter with Pilate:

> "When Pilate heard this, he was even more afraid and he asked Jesus, "Where do you come from?", but Jesus gave no answer. "Do you refuse to speak to me?" Pilate said, "Do you not realise that I have the power to either free you or crucify you?". Jesus answered, "You would have no power over me if it were not given to you from above."" (John 19)

> "Courage is not the absence of fear, but the assessment that something else is more important than fear." (Franklin D Roosevelt)

15
Suffering

The brutal reality is that life is not fair. In fact for some people life is even worse – it is cruel, harsh and short. If we are prepared to look, we can see this reality everywhere. Some people are born with severe intellectual and physical handicaps, some people suffer great hardships because of accident and disease, some parents lose beloved children at early ages. The list of human suffering and despair is endless, yet this is one thing we all have in common: we will all suffer.

What we make of that suffering and how we master its consequences are the great questions of life. It is also the great symbol of what you will do with your own life. Human beings have come up with many responses to life's difficulties. Some imagine it is all an illusion; some put their hope in technology, science and medicine; some put their hope in political systems to balance this unfairness; others hope that future genetics will somehow solve the dilemma.

Most Australians however, will have none of these reactions. More likely is a response that recognizes the truth of our circumstances but then proceeds to ignore its consequences. You can hear this clearly in the way we often talk about our lives, "I deserve better than this", "Why did this happen to me?", "My parents don't understand me", "If I win Tattslotto this will solve all my problems", "If I meet Mr/Mrs Right I will be happy", "I will join a gym next year and get fit". The truth is we then proceed to do nothing about these circumstances. We float back to a position that suggests change is impossible as these things belong in a 'too hard basket'.

Dolores was an unusual person in that she noticed suffering. Sometimes it even appeared that she was especially drawn to those who were in the midst of suffering or hardship. Perhaps it was because of her own extreme ill health and long-term battles with several aggressive cancers and related consequences.

In 1981 Dolores, as a 25-year-old, was diagnosed with Non-Hodgkin's Lymphoma. She was one of Australia's early survivors of this disease yet it took a terrible toll on her general health. Radiotherapy in 1981 was in its infancy and many of Dolores' vital organs were severely damaged. In the early 2000s she developed cervical cancer, rectal cancer, two poorly functioning heart valves, and suffered the removal of her thyroid gland and part of her lymphatic system. Increasingly, 'good' days became hard to sustain and management of diverse medications with severe side effects became a logistical difficulty.

For the last 11 years of her life, she was constantly sick and in constant pain, to the point of not being able to climb stairs or undertake short walks. Nevertheless, her attitude to such suffering always revealed a depth of humility and wider concern not to be a burden. Throughout this period, she continued to work, insisted on doing her own housework, and refused to talk about - or allow me to tell others about - her medical issues. This was always focused on both not troubling others but also wishing to maintain her personal integrity. She did not want others to feel sorry for her, believing incredibly that her problems were not as complex or as severe as some others.

She was extremely ill more than a decade, but to her credit, very few knew this, and she remained the person for others, the first one to see others in hospital, the first to ring or visit. Throughout these painful and suffering years she never deviated in her concern for others.

For me, her saintliness is confirmed, as I saw how hard her life was, but I also witnessed her endless prayers for others at the side of her bed, her unwavering devotion to Our Lady and the saints and her profound care for myself. I do not know why but I remained her number one concern each and every day of our life together.

16
Culture

Dolores was rightly proud of her Italian background and cultural heritage. Naturally hers was the best Italian cooking available. Indeed she usually banned us from going to Italian restaurants on the grounds that she could make Italian food better and she was correct!

Dolores could easily identify and appreciate the nature of Italian architecture, Italianate churches, historical artefacts, but she could also be saddened by the state of modern Italy, the pervasiveness of the Mafia influence in the South and the loss of drive and purpose shown by many people living in modern Italy.

Nevertheless, for Dolores, she was first and foremost an Australian who loved this country above all others. For Dolores, Australia had delivered to her family a level of wealth, security and reward for effort not found in Europe. She identified strongly with values of hard work, strong family, community loyalty and a desire to succeed.

For much of her life Dolores worked two jobs: yes, a centralised office job, but then she layered this with nannying, house cleaning, extra typing or shopping for the housebound. There was no work that she was not prepared to do and she often noted to me that this was the reason she had been able to afford her first property, a small two-bedroom apartment in North Adelaide. She was always proud of this achievement, indeed often believing it to be a kind of miracle; that a small, uneducated Italian girl could manage to purchase her own property in what for her was 'wealthy' Australia.

Notwithstanding these expressions of love for country and hard work, Dolores also had two far deeper understandings of what culture should mean and how it was activated. For her, 'personal culture' was at the forefront of who you were and the basis of what you brought to your family, friends, and the wider Australian society. This culture, your personal culture, is witnessed in your actions and behaviours every day of the week, by everyone you meet. For Dolores your personal culture is one of the most important things you own and largely determines your success or otherwise in the world, particularly in the workplace but also in your personal life.

Disappointingly, many Australians imagine that their behaviours and actions are not seen by others or they have the rather strange view that others must accept their behaviours and actions at face value. The mantra that 'this is who I am' and that others must 'accept me, warts and all' is the mantra of a failed individual. The truth is vastly different; no one has to accept anything about you and people will quickly determine whether you are a person they wish to know or include in their lives.

The difficulty for individuals who imagine that others must 'adapt' to them is that they have forgotten that actions and behaviours are 'matters of choice'. When we understand that our 'culture' towards others is a matter of choice, then we can appreciate the value of being our best for others.

The world is full of mediocre people who do not bring excellence to their personal interactions with others. These are the people who constantly expect you to adapt to their needs but have little concept of doing something for others, without it being seen as a significant burden. Dolores never made the mistake of imagining that these behaviours are not seen or taken note of.

Dolores acted in a different way; she developed a personal culture of excellence, rightly believing that it acted creatively and pastorally in the lives of others. A word of encouragement, a small act of generosity, a willingness to share a burden of others can make a profound difference to the lives of others. And all it requires of us is a small amount of time and the ability to 'see' others; offering to help someone with a small job or driving another to an appointment are opportunities to transform the lives of others.

Dolores never took these things lightly; they were always opportunities to offer others an 'extraordinary culture' and, in her own way, make the world a better place.

For Dolores, you did not need to 'do' great things to be an extraordinary person. You just needed to bring excellence into the ordinary things of life that most of us overlook.

> "No one is useless in this world who lightens the burden of others." (Charles Dickens)
>
> "We make a living by what we get; we make a life by what we give." (Winston Churchill)
>
> "For it is in giving that we receive." (St Francis of Assisi)

17
The Beauty of Tradition

There is significant anxiety in modern Australia regarding the many difficulties our nation appears to be facing. If we follow our media to any degree it would be easy to conclude we are a nation beset by crises.

We have a pandemic crisis, an economic crisis, fuel shortages, supply problems, lack of workers, home ownership problems and in many of our cities, poor roads, rail and other infrastructure issues. On a social and community level we appear surrounded by alcohol and drug issues, a marriage crisis, a sexual abuse crisis, a significant decline in Christian religious observation, unhappy Indigenous Australians, a shortage of teachers, nurses, doctors and priests, with a new crisis in mental health amongst many of our fellow Australians.

The solutions to many of these problems

appear insurmountable, yet increasingly commentators, politicians, bishops, and community leaders are ramping up calls for change and the abandonment of many of our traditions, and of course increased funding for particular projects believed to offer the ability to solve various problems.

For Dolores, most of these societal and personal difficulties stemmed from a lack of vocation and identity. That is, people have no idea what God has called them to do. For the majority of Australians our work and leisure time is focused only inwards: What do we want? What makes us happy? The concept that some part of our lives should be set apart in the service of others and of God is an alien idea to most Australians. Rightly, Dolores saw this self-orientation as the basis of all of our other problems, particularly those to do with lack of resilience and mental health stresses.

Dolores subscribed to two particular ideas of St Augustine: firstly, that "God has made each of us for himself and that our hearts are restless until they find their rest in God", therefore we are called to think and ponder on the things that God requires of us; and secondly, a more underlying idea, Dolores believed with St Augustine "that to fall in love with God is the greatest romance, to seek Him the greatest adventure, to find Him the greatest human achievement".

For Dolores, as it is for all Catholics, the vehicle for falling in love with God was the vehicle of Church teaching and tradition. Tradition was never obsolete for Dolores or worthless as it is for some 'sophisticated Australians'; rather it was the gift of God that allowed us to love without measure and to correct and shape our disordered and self-centred minds and spirits.

For Dolores, tradition was not something to be kept within a church but something to be spread to others. There was never any need to defend it; it was only a case of letting it loose, and it would defend itself. Many people regularly suggested to Dolores that the Church should change, should adapt or modernise itself to the spirit of the Age. She always found this a great confusion and mistake. Since she had become married to me, she adopted Essendon as her football team. I was under no illusion she actually liked the club, but she saw it as part of an effort to share her husband's interests and add another layer of communication to our life.

To all of those who constantly suggested the Church was out of date, Dolores would suggest their club should change their mascot or colours. So, would you be happy to abandon the Blues, Bombers, Tigers or Demons to become something more Australian like the 'Possums' and change team jumpers to shades of green and gold?

This suggestion was always met with outrage; indeed, most people inherently knew that these two simple changes to colours and mascots would fundamentally destroy their clubs. All said they would no longer attend games, buy memberships or support these clubs. These traditions are usually less than a century old, yet we are not prepared to undertake such changes because the essence of those clubs would be different.

Yet, people who do not attend mass suggest the Church needs to change 2000 years of 'workable' history and tradition. Dolores knew if you wish to kill something you abandon tradition. For Dolores, Catholic tradition remained seriously radical. Her tradition was a constant and unchanging theme, guided by church teaching. God is with you, God won't abandon you, God is for you. For Dolores God was a God of loyalty, constant loyalty.

All of this came from her experience but also her knowledge of tradition, the day-to-day experience of God, the God who fulfilled his promises. In Dolores' view you did not attend mass because you had to; it was a form of gratefulness for what God had done for her. Hers was not a faith of changing the Church to suit herself, but changing herself to suit what God had already done.

So what were the traditions that Dolores kept? For Dolores tradition was the answer to vocation – what am I to do for God? Firstly, devotion to Mary was Dolores' mission – that was always the action part:

> Step 1: Get on your knees and pray for those whom you knew were in need of your prayers.
>
> Step 2: Visit them, ring them, talk to them, ask how they are going, let them know that she cared and that, through her, God cared for them as well.

Step 3: Check in regularly, follow up and continue the journey with them.

For Dolores caring, praying and loving were never a one-off experience. In the same way God is consistent, so was Dolores. All of this was the vocation and mission of loving you. Dolores did not have to agree with you, yet underneath she knew God was calling you and that your ultimate happiness depended on your response.

In practical terms, to meet Dolores was to undertake a journey, a gentle journey but one that was ultimately driven by God, not her. She absolutely lived the teaching of Jesus: "Come to me, all who are weary and burdened and I will give you rest. Take my yoke upon you and learn from me, for I am gentle and humble in heart and you will find rest for your souls, for my yoke is easy and my burden is light." (Matthew II, 28-30)

Unfortunately, in modern Australia, too many of us elect to give up, too many of us act as though we are powerless, tired, stressed or just go to bed. Every day you will hear endless complaints of others or you will hear that someone else or the Government should fix the problem. We must be realistic about these 'words' and what they really mean. They are the language of people who cannot fix their own lives and have little to offer you in yours.

The truth lies elsewhere and is seen in the life of Dolores and others who do. It does not matter what happens to you in life, it does not matter what your background is. The great question is: what will you do with what you have been given? It is certainly true that life is not fair or easy and that sometimes the future looks blank, yet the example of Dolores is clear – no excuses: don't talk, do!

> "Tradition is not the worship of ashes, but the preservation of fire." (Gustav Mahler)

> "A love of tradition has never weakened a nation or individual, indeed it has strengthened them in their hour of need." (Winston Churchill)

> "The pursuit of knowledge for its own sake, the fanatical love of justice and the desire for personal freedom – these are the features of tradition and I thank God that I belong to it." (Albert Einstein)

18
Prayer:
Small Steps – Lasting Impact

Many people consider prayer a difficult undertaking, one that is sometimes arduous, and often fails to produce the results we desire or think we deserve. Dolores never thought like this; she kept prayer short and non-demanding. Prayer was a series of short conversations about all sorts of things. She did not really ask God for things, she just chatted, and no doubt it was a little like all her conversations – this happened today, so and so said such and such, now what do you think we should do about it? God was a friend with whom you just walked and talked and, like conversations with our friends, most things would not be resolved with one chat … so I will talk to you again in the morning!

Nevertheless, Dolores had a few major understandings about prayer. Ultimately the decisions would be made by God. She did not really dream big; her prayer concerns surrounded small, simple, achievable ideas. How could the exam results go? How would my sister's or aunt's or brother's problems be resolved? How could another person be made to feel happier or make a positive change in life? All these prayers were small, bite-size, achievable concerns – genuine and earnestly sought, believing that God would accomplish good things yet they were overwhelmingly small, and focused on others. For Dolores, God worked in small ways, but then Everest is reached by thousands of little steps. This is how Dolores prayed.

In my work I get to hear the aspirations of many young Australians. I've heard of dreams of space flight, of climbing Everest, of building great wealth, of playing test cricket, or one of first grade football in one of any number of codes. I have also heard of less outwardly complicated dreams that may involve weight loss, quitting smoking, learning a language or playing an instrument.

Nevertheless, for many people that is what the dream remains – a topic of conversation with little link to reality. It is sad to hear individuals explain their great love of animals and their dream of becoming a vet, to discover that they have no desire to return to school or that they reject or do not like study. The same applies to those who wish to be sports stars yet acknowledge that their physical fitness is poor and that they have no plans to engage in a training routine.

For many people the disconnection between 'life-goal' and the method for reaching this goal is worlds apart. Such goals have become little more than a delusion, or a fairy story designed to entertain others. Deep down many people know that such a disconnection exists; that is why another layer of conversation is never far behind. This conversation concerns all the reasons and excuses that we have failed to begin the journey to our goal. These will be things like "I don't have enough time", "The timing is not right", "I'm waiting for someone to help me", or "I don't have enough money".

Yet, the reality remains – many of us have just pushed our dreams and goals further into the future, to a time or place where they will never be achieved. The reality that nothing worth having is ever easy, or that some goals will require diligence or toughness becomes the subconscious excuse for not beginning.

Dolores thought that these stresses and excuses could also exist in people's minds in relation to prayer and even something as simple as returning to mass. Dolores came upon many people who expressed their desire to reconnect with God and with his church but often things surrounding family, work or time restraints seemed to get in the way.

Dolores was always very gentle and encouraging with such views. She always encouraged the reality of a small step process: begin with a short prayer now, don't wait until next year to commence, ask for a little gift for someone else, get out of the way and let God do his work. For Dolores it was never the case of worrying about an unachievably large goal, but rather not being afraid to ask for something small and simple that can be done today!

For Dolores taking a small prayer step was infinitely better than promising to return to mass next year. For her, doing a little led to a lot. Dolores in her own small way was able to replenish the advice of St Paul who noted:

> "We have this treasure in clay jars, so that it may be made clear that this extraordinary power belongs to God and does not come from us. We are afflicted in every way but not crushed, perplexed but not driven to despair, persecuted but not forsaken, struck down but not destroyed, always carry in our bodies the death of Jesus, so that the life of Jesus may also be made visible." (2 Corinthians 4, 7-10)

Certainly Dolores could be afflicted and perplexed by life. Sometimes some individuals bullied and persecuted her, particularly in workplaces, yet she was never crushed or driven to despair. Each day offered a new beginning and a new opportunity to make a small but lasting difference. Dolores knew that some days could be hard but she was also a strong believer that God's purposes were good, that change was possible in even the most obnoxious individuals and that her task was to bring their little problems, stresses, arrogance or failings before God.

This was not done in either distress or superiority; she just thought that God had brought these issues to her as 'talking points'. She never failed to bring these 'problem' people before God because that was her task. Small continuous prayers for everyone were her central motto. Dolores subscribed to the idea that beauty and goodness, like blooming flowers, were available to each of us, but firstly we had to understand our seeds grow out of the dirt.

19
Why go to Mass?

Mass attendance in modern Australia is seriously struggling. Certainly the cares of the world, the 'busy-ness' of modern life, the need to commit time to parents or children or wider friends can all be used as 'reasonable' excuses to put off going to mass on a regular basis. It is also highly likely that the 'experience' of mass may not always be uplifting - joke-telling priests who place their own personality at the centre of the liturgy, poor music, boring sermons and a lifeless atmosphere were all things that annoyed Dolores at mass but these were never reasons she would consider using to not attend.

For some Catholics, going to mass is a highly developed habit sometimes overlaid by guilt or a sense of duty. These were never the reasons that Dolores used to compel herself to attend mass. Dolores always went to mass for a single reason. She visited to say 'thank you' for the many gifts and benefits that she had received from God in the course of her week. Gratitude was the central engrossing reason for her presence at mass each week. For Dolores, talking to God and thanking him for his constant benefits to her was always a life giving experience. Not only did she actively remember the saving death of Jesus in the mass, but she layered her gratefulness to include her parents, her friends, her husband, people she had encountered during the week, those she knew to be hurting or suffering, those angry or frustrated, those experiencing loss, and those who were happy or joyous.

The whole gamut of the human experience was brought in gratefulness before God. Mass for Dolores was never about her needs or worries. It was not a quest to somehow feel better, it was not about receiving benefits of peace or acceptance (although this usually occurred), it was never about easing pain or gaining energy to confront difficult weeks ahead. These things never entered her thoughts or heart. Her mass experience was totally bound up in bringing others before God, so that they might experience something of the love, security and joy she received, especially in her devotion to the mother of Jesus and the mercy she could bestow.

I witnessed her constantly on her knees before statues of Our Lady, constantly lighting candles for the needs of others and constantly returning to church to light one more candle or say one more prayer for someone she had forgotten.

Dolores seemed to instinctively know that mass was not to be endured or suffered through, but that it was an opportunity to welcome someone else into the love and hospitality of God. Mass was a ministry she was called to share with others, even if they never knew of those intentions. Dolores never spoke much about God to others but she 'actioned' it every week. Perhaps that is the fundamental reason people identified Dolores as different. Actions always came before words.

20
What God is like – Dolores' View

For both Dolores and I one of the great places to visit is the southern states of America – Louisiana, Alabama, Mississippi. In those states the first question they ask you is not "What work do you do?" which is a very Australian question, but "Where do your people come from?" In fact the greatest insult a Southerner has for a Northerner (whom they call Yankees) is that the people up north are "not from anywhere"!

For a Southerner, you cannot trust a person who does not know their family history; you cannot trust a person who does not know stories about their parents, uncles, aunts, grandparents – what they did, what they overcame and who they were – because in knowing them, they know you!! Dolores felt there was a lot of truth in this idea, particularly as, for her, her parents' journey from Italy and their struggles and success in Australia was fundamentally her story as well.

Unfortunately, the Australian Catholic Church has a lot of problems in this area. Dolores would go to many parishes and always be disappointed to discover that no-one knew their parish histories, no-one knew the battles they overcame to establish the Church, no-one could find a good news story to promote as a unifying or bonding story.

Like Southern Americans, she felt if you have no stories, if you have no foundational myth, if you have no history, then you have no culture and you have no future. In Dolores' view, therein lies the problem for the Catholic Church - if you cannot tell your own stories then someone else will tell them for you. Often these can be overwhelmingly negative.

In fact the only current story told by others about the Catholic Church in modern Australia is one of 'abuse'. For Dolores, we have lost the ability to connect with wider Australia, Catholics no longer seem able to influence our society, we do not seem to be able to help people to get over their failures, or show them how to make a life – for in Dolores' view we no longer tell stories. In truth, modern Australia gets its wisdom, truth and advice from Google – not from Catholicism. This is the great challenge for the Australian church: How do we again learn to speak to Australia? How do we again bring the great things we offer, not only to each other but to our society? How do we tell good news stories about our faith?

In the view of Dolores, storytelling was a natural event, but this was never about evangelizing or converting others. All of her stories were natural and truthful yet, ever so gently, she would speak of God's action in her life – always in the view of "I have so much to be grateful for". For Dolores, God was not distant, he was not hands-off, he was not a psychological phenomenon – he was a friend who played a part in every dimension of her life. This was not done stupidly, as some Catholics do – God did not help Dolores find carparks! – but stories about God helping her parents, her sister, her brother, and brother-in-law. God's participation in the life of Dolores was as natural as breathing. God was there – you talked and chatted to him and he was able to change and improve things – not always the way you thought things should go, but always for the better.

Both Dolores and I considered our marriage to be an event like that. Indeed we thought that was the key action of God in our lives and we orientated our actions to each other in the knowledge that this was a truth – a gift given to us – but one which also needed our strength and our participation.

For Dolores, God did not act alone – he expected us to be his partner in the undertakings we did as a married couple. This was never a 'slavish' or unthinking view but as a genuine 'structure' that bonded us together. God walked alongside our relationship and fully participated in our lives.

Dolores had a strong desire to do the 'right' thing; she was occasionally motivated to 'talk' to Archbishops and Bishops, particularly if she thought they were not doing what God had entrusted them to do. This was most strongly witnessed in her devotion to St James Brighton. I clearly remember a distraught Dolores who had gone to work early, ringing me as she passed the already burning church and we both witnessed her beloved church fully ablaze long before the fire brigade had arrived. What was to unfold in coming years was truly shocking.

After but a few months, it became obvious that the Archbishop had 'bought' into a false narrative around the fire being justice for the actions of a 'pedophile' priest some 25 years earlier. The later appointment of a new parish priest, adamant that the church should not be rebuilt, caused deep pain and long-lasting animosities.

Dolores was fully aware that a beautiful statue of Our Lady of Lourdes had miraculously survived the fire, only to mysteriously 'disappear' after its removal from the site. When she inquired of the parish priest to its whereabouts, she was told clearly that she needed to let go of her old-fashioned superstitions and devotion to Our Lady. And so began the long and ultimately successful 'Save -and restore St James' Committee. These individuals deserve high praise for the reconstruction of that beautiful and special church in the face or rigorous and malicious opposition from those in positions of authority. Doing the 'right' thing is costly – those early committee members have suffered greatly but are a 'good news' example of simple Catholics doing the work of God in 21st Century Australia. For Dolores, God was not only a natural part of family history but of

St James history, indeed a central and reliable partner.

> "I will not leave you as orphans, I will come to you. In a little while the world will see me no more but you will see me. Because I live, you also will live."
> (John 14:18)

For Dolores, this is our family history – this is God telling us what he will be doing and how he will be there for us – even when he is no longer physically present.

Dolores was greatly concerned with the difficulties of younger Australians. Unquestionably, they are under great stress and enticement in regard to social issues. The impact of drugs, mental health, alcohol, depression, anxiety, family breakdown, unemployment and crime have resulted in increasing numbers of young Australians finding it hard to integrate into society and make a meaningful contribution to it.

Young Australians have higher rates of depression and seek medical and psychological treatment at levels not seen previously in our national history. This state of affairs is not new and has been unfolding for perhaps the last 25-30 years. It does appear that neither our educational or medical experts have answers that are viable or effective.

Dolores was a great believer in taking charge of your own life, but that was always under the wider umbrella of God. She believed that a number of important questions needed to be asked of ourselves if we are to shape our lives in beneficial ways. These are all internal questions that must be answered by each individual and cannot be avoided or passed to others – Why am I here? What is the purpose of my life? What is the meaning of life? What am I meant to do with my life? – and the really essential question, "What does God want me to undertake for him?"

The truth of Australian society is that these questions are not fully considered or that the answers given only contain partial truth. Certainly it is possible to mask internal emptiness through many of the solutions we employ but the questions remain and only the symptoms are partially blocked. Clearly, drugs, alcohol or anti-depressants can distract or temporarily make individuals feel secure and comfortable. But the impact is short-lived, the questions remain and the costs to our bodies and souls is often damaging.

In my profession I deal with a substantial number of people who are considering suicide. In my view, no individual considers such an act when the 'why' questions of life have been answered effectively. In the same way, continued drug or alcohol use always has its base unanswered questions about 'Who am I?' and 'What is the meaning of my life?'

Dolores subscribed to the famous maxim of St Augustine, "Our hearts are restless until they rest in God".

The parable of the Prodigal Son was one of Dolores' favourite parables, because at its most basic level it spoke of God's actions and relationships as part of a family. This parable tells the story of a lost son who demands his inheritance from his father, leaves home and then squanders the money in a life of recklessness. With nothing left of his inheritance he is forced to work in filthy jobs just to survive and finally he determines to return to his father, beg forgiveness and ask for a servant role. The response of the father was the very essence of the faith for Dolores.

> "So he set off and went to his father. But while he was still far off his father saw him and was filled with compassion; he ran and put his arms around him and kissed him. Then the son said to him, "Father, I have sinned against heaven and before you; I am no longer worthy to be called your son". But the father said to his slaves, "Quickly bring out a robe, the best one – and put it on him; put a ring on his finger and sandals on his feet. And get the fattest calf and kill it, for this son of mine was dead and is alive again, he was lost and now he is found" and they began to celebrate" (Luke 15: 20-24).

This story fits perfectly with all that Dolores knew about God. God's love does not depend on our faithfulness, it is unconditional, he loves us when we are still far off. This was the experience and the action of Dolores. Yes, she could be hurt often by others but she was always willing to forgive and open herself to us in new ways. She was a person of second chances and did we all not benefit from that attitude.

21
The Communion of Saints: Praying to and with Dolores

For most Australians, and perhaps even most Catholics, stories, pictures and discussions about the saints evoke images of perfect people who have achieved high levels of sanctity, or performed miraculous deeds. For most of us this would appear to be a club few of us could hope to join. Whilst this understanding is not totally incorrect, the view that Dolores held of saints is much more accurate. She held the saints, both living and dead, as a group of friends whom you could call upon to participate in your life and offer you help, companionship or advice through both difficult and joyous times of life. For Dolores, the saints were not there to 'fix' things but to engage with us in connection and unity. The saints for Dolores were like family you could call upon to discuss all sorts of issues. They made up a part of the Church that helped you and shared your spiritual journey.

In the eyes of Dolores all Christians, living and dead, were part of a community that upheld and stood for the truth, no matter what our current circumstances. In talking to the saints, Dolores experienced encouragement, compassion, support, wisdom and love. For Dolores, the Church was not defined by its power, bishops or priests but by its service, bearing each other's burdens, standing for the truth and being honest and loyal. For Dolores, the Church was a communion of people she could call upon. She had many favourite saints but perhaps the most important was St Anthony of Padua who, on a basic level, is perceived as the patron saint of lost things. So whilst Dolores regularly prayed to St Anthony for lost keys or other items, she was much more profound in her understanding of St Anthony. Her connection with St Anthony was mostly in regard to lost peoples, those who had lost their faith, or those whose life appeared to be in turmoil or trouble. I can attest to many, many conversations with Dolores, where she would note with complete understatement that St Anthony had indeed rectified or changed the life of one of her friends, acquaintances or just someone in need. Dolores was in no doubt that St Anthony was a powerful figure in making the lives of others stronger and more faithful.

The Catechism of the Catholic church notes, "Being more closely united to Christ, those who dwell in heaven fix the whole church more firmly in holiness ... they do not cease to intercede with the father for us, as they proffer the merits which they acquired on Earth through the one mediator between God and men, Christ Jesus." (Catechism No. 956).

As the husband of Dolores I was fortunate beyond my dreams to encounter a wife and friend who gave her total self to our life and relationship. And whilst I continue to be missing her beauty, her companionship and her love every day, I also know that through the communion of saints she continues to be connected to me and guiding me in unique ways. The connection is now eternal. And so I would encourage all who knew her and those who need some help in life to pray and chat with Dolores, and be not afraid to ask for her guidance her refreshment and encouragement.

> "Praying for others is a sign of love and the more love the saints in heaven have the more they pray for those on Earth who can be helped by their prayers." (St

Thomas Aquinas)

"Let us become saints for each other, so that having been together on Earth, we can be together in Heaven." (St Padre Pio)

22
Catholicism: The Family Faith

Dolores was deeply drawn to Catholicism because for her it was "the family faith". Dolores loved the idea of praying to saints and asking the saints for daily help. This was absolutely no different from ringing her sister to discuss an issue or talking to her husband, cousins, neighbors or work colleagues. The saints were family, acted like family and got treated as valued family members. This is an absolutely Catholic idea which Dolores upheld; saints were special, not necessarily because they had done great things but because God had called them to this status. This is absolutely the view of the Bible. In Romans, St Paul refers to "All God's beloved in Rome, who are called to be saints" (Romans 1-17) and later in Corinthians, he speaks of "all the Churches of the saints" (1 Corinthians 14:33). For Dolores saints did not necessarily include bishops, priests, healers or miracle workers in any obvious way. The saints were faithful and holy because God had made them so. In the same way God had come to share our life in the incarnation, the birth of Jesus to Mary at Christmas, so our true family home was for us to be part of the divine family. Dolores agreed absolutely with St Paul who said "We share God's holiness because we are in Christ and with St Peter who said "We have become partakers of the divine nature." (2 Peter, 1-4)

Now that Dolores has entered into her eternal life, she also has joined the saints, the communion of our friends and loved ones in Heaven.

Dolores had something more profound and important than personal or private achievements. She had a drive and an orientation that was totally and utterly for others: Dolores was a saint for others. Her inner life, her prayer life, her fundamental concerns were never about herself, that is what struck so many people in such an overwhelming and profound way. She was always focused on the needs, hopes, dreams and concerns of others. If sainthood has anything to do with self-forgetfulness and the tender care and concern for others, then Dolores is one of our greatest Australian saints. Her private life was not easy. She knew significant suffering, pain and distress. Yet she trusted in God and Our Lady to always be at her side and to get her through all her difficulties. She entrusted her own life to them, which allowed her to get on with thinking about and helping others.

Dolores walked boldly the Via Dolorosa, ironically the root of the name her parents gave her. She had no pretence, no self-pity, no bluster or hostility towards others – only the desire to love and help them. Her life is a profound one with much to offer us all, the path to being a happy and successful person but much more importantly the path to eternal life. After I had finished the eulogy for her Adelaide funeral, the priest celebrating the mass, Fr James, got up and summarized my words in one sentence, "If you want to see God, do what Dolores did".

23
Dolores: Our Family Saint

The Catholic Church has taught the beauty of praying with and to the saints since the beginning. It has always formed part of the Church's fundamental teaching and the Apostles' Creed from the 5th Century states succinctly, "We believe in the communion of saints". So Catholicism is a faith that prays for one another and asks prayers for each other. Nor does the Church teach that death has disconnected us from the ones we love. In fact the Church teaches that we were made to live in the communion of saints and for Catholics interpersonal relationships do not end with death. The Roman missal makes this absolutely clear, "Indeed for your faithful Lord, life is changed not ended and when this earthly dwelling turns to dust, an eternal dwelling is made ready for them in Heaven".

It is entirely normal to ask Dolores to pray for us, to pray to her and to ask her for her help. This is how we should be living our lives. Dolores is not absent or missing from our lives; indeed in God's view he has blessed her and brought her to the fullness of eternal life for our benefit and for our imitation. God wants us to keep good company and we can have no better company than Dolores. When we stay close to her, we stay close to God. When we imitate her, we imitate God. As St John tells us in Revelation, "Blessed are those who die in the Lord and blessed are those invited to the marriage supper of the Lord." (Rev 14.13-19.9) This is indeed the role that God has outlined for Dolores. The work of Dolores is to bring us to immortality.

24
Via Dolorosa:
Look After My James

In truth there is a great deal in the life of Dolores I am unable to comprehend. Although I am a Catholic priest who sees suffering and dying every day, it is entirely different when this suffering revolves around and through someone you love. So there is a part of me that is disappointed in God, a part of me that feels that Dolores did not receive a fair chance at life, a part of me that prayed desperately for resurrection. All I wanted was to have my wife live – yet that view of resurrection and healing was not forthcoming.

I would not wish the years and years of illness upon anyone nor would I wish anyone to experience the desperation and chaos of being with loved ones dependent on life support, being placed in a coma, of diagnoses ranging from minor brain injury to catastrophic intellectual impairment, to then seeing the miracle of consciousness return and recognition acknowledged, only to have this removed again through a final breakdown of heart and lung capacity.

I am not a priest who criticises Catholics who have separated themselves from the Church or who find that their faith is sometimes lukewarm; my experience is perhaps similar. Sometimes if you wrestle with God you get injured and sometimes our faith can be so damaged in hurt that it is hard to restart again. I thought these things often and although I clung to God, it was often in desperation and fear. I was happy to accept anything as long as I did not lose my Dolores.

This was not how Dolores looked at her life; hers was a much more peaceful and reconciled view of life. As I clung on in desperation, she organised others to look after me, knowing she did not have long to live. I continued to refuse to see such an eventuality. Dolores peacefully prepared for it.

The Catechism of the Catholic Church tries to explain the role of suffering in human life. I know this as truth on an intellectual level, but Dolores knew this in her heart and soul.

> "Moved by so much suffering, Christ not only allowed himself to be touched by the sick, but he made their miseries his own. He took our infirmities and bore our diseases". But he did not heal all the sick. His healings were signs of the coming of the Kingdom of God. They announced a more radical healing: the victory over our sin and death through his Passover. On the cross Christ took upon himself the whole weight of evil and took away the sin of the world, of which illness is only a consequence. By his passion and death on the cross Christ has given a new meaning to suffering. It can henceforth configure us to him and unite us with his redemptive passion."
> (Catechism 1505)

This is undoubtedly how Dolores saw her life. She was absolutely the woman for others but on a whole other level she was actively bringing about the Kingdom of God. One small step at a time, she configured her life with Christ to the point where she knew her own suffering to be for the benefit of others. I hope this will be her greatest gift to her family and friends – she lived, she suffered and ultimately gave her life for others. Her greatest purpose was ultimately directed at her husband as she regularly said to me, "I don't know why God sent me to you, but I know my job is to fix you and make you a better priest". I always thought she was joking; perhaps this is becoming a firm reality at last.

25

Miraculum Dolores

The Catholic Church has a rigorous and specific understanding of what constitutes a miracle. This is almost always related to a lasting remission of a serious life-threatening medical condition. This is an entirely natural and reasonable position to hold and there are many people in our world in desperate need and hope for healing who live with indescribable pain and restrictions to their life. Turning to God for a change in these circumstances can be a great benefit and is reflected in the great many healings that have occurred through the love and actions of God, particularly those that bring new life into lives of great suffering and which were unexpected or impossible within modern medical frameworks.

Dolores had a much wider and deeper definition of a miracle. She held that miracles were actions of God that always showed others how much God loved them. These were actions and interventions of God that took away suffering and primarily changed lives into new and positive directions. For Dolores, miracles were events, conversations, movements or actions that showed the power and authenticity of God in everyday events of people's lives. Miracles were things that led to small changes but changes that really changed lives and made a difference to the everyday blockages that we all have in life.

Dolores did extraordinary and miraculous things to the lives of others. She brought gentleness to the angry, peace to the anxious, care and concern to those without hope. To some she stimulated the discovery of a new way of living, for others a strength or assurance that they were on the right path.

This was never a gift she claimed for herself. Jesus and Mary were the only ones that acted within the life of the individual, but Dolores was certainly called to help with the de-cluttering so that the individuals concerned could see and respond to new futures and pathways. Those pathways did not come from her but from the calling and quiet whispers of Jesus and Our Lady in showing and opening new paths.

For Dolores, the miracles of God always brought peace, joy, assurance, strength and most importantly 'truth', for they were based on the actions of God in our lives and they changed people who had lost hope. For Dolores miracles were constant, everywhere in all lives and obvious to those who took the time to see.

For some Catholics miracles are completely at the direction of God and this is certainly true, in that the 'deserving' or 'right' to a miracle has little to do with the behaviour or humility of the human individual. God has directed miracles to the greatest sinners, to cruel and hurtful individuals and to those who remain ungrateful even after changes in health or remission of serious illness.

Yet, for Dolores, these utterly undeserving actions of God were not the real miracle to be found. The real miracle was to be found in the human acceptance, the human change. For Dolores real miracles required both divine and human action and the greatest aspect of the miracle was the human change. For Dolores understood how stubborn, arrogant and indifferent humans really are. The greatest of God's miracles are always found in the human change that results from the action of God.

There is a mountain of evidence and individual anecdotes and stories that suggest that Dolores is having a huge impact on people from beyond the grave. People have had their life changed just by listening to the story of Dolores and by understanding that there might be another way to live your life.

I know people who have simply worn her clothes, heard something of the kind of person she was and have taken on a renewed determination to retrieve something in life, such as get a first job or achieve a goal. Just the identification with Dolores from the simple process of wearing her clothes has made a huge change in some lives. Already at this point, three months after her death there are six people who have worn her clothes and now achieved regular work, where previously they had none. There are also individuals who have had deeply troubled relationships with their parents and, listening to the gratefulness that Dolores showed towards her parents, have made changes to their relationships with their parents. This has resulted in new ways that parents, children and loved ones actually form into families. These are miracles because they tap into something of the life and spirit of Dolores, but they also put us into the hands of God.

The miracles that Dolores concerned herself with did not just happen. They were wrestled and fought over and Dolores prayed hard for all those whose lives she adopted in some way. For Dolores, God is a God of engagement, a God who loves humans and loves to get down in the mud and wrestle with humans – and yes, sometimes in wrestling God, there is injury and hurt or lack of understanding or hope. Yet for Dolores, God's outcomes would always prove to be the best ones!

In her own life Dolores did not receive healing. She had half her adult life consumed by cancers, illness, pain and restrictions. Yet she received and passed on to others something more miraculous and more powerful – the ability to change another person's life through a word or example, but mostly a moment of compassion and attentiveness.

Dolores was influenced by one particular parable of Jesus that she put into action every day and that can be undertaken by all of us.

"On one occasion an expert in the Law stood up to Jesus. "Teacher" he asked, what must I do to inherit eternal life? What is written in the Law, how do you read it?" He answered, "Love the Lord your God with all your heart and soul, with all your strength and with all you mind, and love your neighbour as yourself". "You have answered correctly", Jesus replied, "Do this and you will live." But he wanted to justify himself, so he asked Jesus, "And who is my neighbour?"

In reply Jesus said, "A man was going down from Jerusalem to Jerico, when he was attacked by robbers. They stripped him of his clothes, beat him and went away, leaving him half dead. A priest happened to be going down the same road, and when he saw the man he passed by on the other side. So too, a Levite, when he came to the place and saw him, passed by on other side. But a Samaritan, as he travelled, came where the man was and when he saw him he took pity on him. He went to him and bandaged his wounds, pouring on oil and wine. Then he put the man on his own donkey, brought him to an inn and took care of him. The next day he took out two denarii and gave them to the innkeeper. "Look after him", he said, "and when I return, I will reimburse you for any extra expenses you may have".

Which of these three do you think was a neighbour to the man who fell into the hands of robbers? The expert of the Law replied, "The one who had mercy on him". Jesus told him, "Go and do likewise".

"Go and do likewise"; therein lies the miracles of Dolores.

> Think this Day will never dawn again
>
> The miracles of God are calling you and wheel around you
>
> Displaying to you their eternal beauties
>
> And still your eye is looking on the ground   (Dante)

26
The Love Of Dolores For Mary

Dolores had a most beautiful devotion to Mary the mother of Jesus. For Dolores, Mary was the key human being in all recorded history. For this simple, poor and unknown girl was the first human, the representative of all of us, to say yes to God.

For Dolores, the greatest words of scripture were the words of Mary "Let it be done to me, according to your word." (Luke 1.38)

Dolores was not the first to love Mary but, along with all the saints, she also understood that to be close to Christ is also to be close to Mary. For Dolores, Jesus had given his life to be our own, he had made us partakers in the divine life, he has given us his home (Heaven) so that we may live in it as well. He has given us his father to be our father and in Mary he has given us his mother. For God to arrange the whole history of humanity to turn on the 'yes' of Mary made her the greatest gift that God has given to each of us. If an unknown girl from a backwater in Palestine can turn history in her humility and love, then Dolores thought, we can do it as well.

This was the model Dolores used – we are co-workers with Mary. Mary was not the end point of human history but the beginning and each of us in Dolores' mind was called to complete human history in service and in love for others. Dolores modelled herself on Mary and thought that none of us could go wrong if life if we did the same.

Dolores viewed Mary as her partner; she walked together with Dolores through life. For Dolores praying with Mary was never hard work; it was just an extension of human conversation and no topic was off limits. Sometimes Dolores would mention that conversations had been vigorous, for devotion to Mary was never slavish but in an authentic partnership. It was honest discussion and working things out. For Dolores her relationship with Mary was peripatetic; it moved, it meandered and sometimes it discovered darkness, fears and obstacles, but none of this worried Dolores because all of it was participation in the life of God.

For Dolores, that's what we are called to be – to be God's partner – and that was always the richest gift she had received, yet one with great responsibility for a devotion to Mary was not to be about our comfort or reassurance but always a call to do, for in the view of Dolores, Mary always called us to costly action in the service of others. For Dolores, her partnership meant vocation, it was not meant to confer comfort but always to stimulate the question, "What do you want me to do?" and then the essential sub-action, "Let it be done to me according to your will".

Devotion to Mary was always vocation and always action-orientated. That meant taking the time to notice people, to say hello, to speak to difficult people, stepping out of your comfort zone – 'going' to others, 'seeing' others, noticing their moods, fears, frustrations or pain and hurt.

For Dolores, devotion to Mary was all about the 'seeing' in like manner to the good Samaritan; it was not about passing on the other side, but stopping, pouring salve on wounds and bandaging. This is the reason so many people noticed Dolores and remarked on the effect she had on them, because she had 'seen' them - in the same way that Our Lady saw Dolores, called her, and does the same to us.

If there was one gift Dolores would want her friends, loved ones, and even those that did not like her to have, it is the gift of devotion to Mary. For in this quiet, unassuming woman from an obscure background we are able to participate in the greatest gifts brought to us by her son Jesus Christ.

27
How To Pray The Rosary: Dolores' Favourite Prayer

The Rosary consists of five decades of Hail Marys. As we pray, each decade we reflect on a particular mystery and a small piece of scripture which gives the prayer its context. All of these Christian mysteries are entirely scriptural and usually highlight one aspect of the life of Jesus. It is not necessary to be a Catholic to say these prayers. Many non-Catholics pray the Rosary. It is also not necessary to complete all of the Rosary prayers in one session. The most important aspect of prayer is to make a start and try to come close to God for a few minutes per day. I have included some prayers linked to the actions and faith of Dolores which I hope may be helpful. Again, it is not necessary to say all these prayers. In Dolores, we have our own particular and unique saint to help us in our devotions. As a person who did not disappoint us in her mortal life, there is no possibility she will disappoint us in our life with God.

The Joyful Mysteries:

1. The Annunciation
2. The Visitation
3. The Nativity
4. The Presentation
5. The finding of the child Jesus in the Temple

The Luminous Mysteries:

1. The Baptism of Christ in the Jordan
2. The Wedding feast at Cana
3. The Proclamation of the Kingdom
4. The Transfiguration of Jesus
5. The Institution of the Eucharist

The Sorrowful Mysteries:

1. The Agony in the Garden
2. The Scourging at the Pillar
3. The Crowning with Thorns
4. The Carrying of the Cross
5. The Crucifixion

The Glorious Mysteries

1. The Resurrection
2. The Ascension
3. The Descent of the Holy Spirit
4. The Assumption of Mary
5. The Coronation of Mary

Prayers of the Rosary

Sign of the Cross

In the name of the Father, of the Son and of the Holy Spirit. Amen

Apostles' Creed

I believe in God, the Father Almighty, creator of Heaven and Earth; and in Jesus Christ, His only Son our Lord, who was conceived by the Holy Spirit, born of the Virgin Mary, suffered under Pontius Pilate, was crucified, died and was buried. He descended into Hell; the third day He rose again from the dead; He ascended into Heaven, and sits at the right hand of God, the Father Almighty; from where He shall come to judge the living and the dead. I believe in the Holy Spirit, the Holy Catholic Church, the communion of saints, the forgiveness of sins, the resurrection of the body, and life everlasting. Amen.

Our Father

Our father, who art in Heaven, hallowed be thy name. Thy Kingdom come, Thy will be done, on Earth as it is in Heaven. Give us this day our daily bread and forgive us our trespasses, as we forgive those who trespass against us. And lead us not into temptation, but deliver us from evil. Amen.

Hail Mary

Hail Mary, full of grace, the Lord is with thee. Blessed art thou among women, and blessed is the fruit of thy womb, Jesus. Holy Mary, Mother of God, pray for us sinners now and at the hour of our death. Amen.

Glory Be

Glory be to the Father, and to the Son and to the Holy Spirit. As it was in the beginning, is now, and ever shall be, world without end. Amen.

Hail Holy Queen

Hail, Holy Queen, mother of Mary, our life our sweetness and our hope. To thee do we cry, poor banished children of Eve; to thee do we send up our sighs, mourning and weeping in this valley of tears. Turn, then, most gracious Advocate, thine eyes of mercy towards us, and after this our exile, show us the blessed fruit of thy womb, Jesus. O clement, O loving, O sweet Virgin Mary.

L: Pray for us, O Holy Mother of God

R: That it may be made worthy of the promises of Christ

Praying the Rosary with Our Lady

The First Joyful Mystery:
Scripture and Prayers
The Annunciation: Luke I, 26-38

In the sixth month of Elizabeth's pregnancy, God sent the Angel Gabriel to Nazareth, a town in Galilee to a virgin pledged to be married to a man named Joseph, a descendant of David. The Virgin's name was Mary. The Angel went to her and said, "Greetings you who are highly favoured! The Lord is with you".

Mary was greatly troubled at his words and wondered what kind of greeting this might be. But the Angel said to her, "Do not be afraid, Mary; you have found favour with God. You will conceive and give birth to a son, and you are to call him Jesus. He will be great and will be called the Son of the most High. The Lord God will give him the throne of his father David, and he will reign over Jacob's descendants forever: and his Kingdom will never end." "How will this be", Mary asked the Angel, "since I am a virgin?" The Angel answered, "The Holy Spirit will come on you, and the power of the most high will overshadow you. So, the one to be born will be called the Son of God. Even Elizabeth, your relative, is going to have a child in her old age, and she who was said to be unable to conceive is in her sixth month. For no word from God will ever fail." "I am the Lord's servant", Mary answered, "May your word to me be fulfilled." Then the Angel left her.

Prayers and Reflections

- Mother Mary, give to us, as you did to Dolores, the patience and humility to see the good in all people, particularly those whom we are tempted to ignore or undervalue. Amen.
- Give to us, Lord Jesus, as you did Dolores, the strength to listen to the stories of the abandoned, rejected, lonely or hurt. Amen.
- Help us Lord to believe, as Dolores did, that no promise that you make to us will ever fail. Amen.
- Pray for us Mary and Dolores, that we may follow God's will in perfect humility. Amen.

Hail Mary, full of grace, the Lord is with thee. Blessed art though amongst women, and blessed is the fruit of thy womb, Jesus. Holy Mary, Mother of God, pray for us sinners now and at the hour of our death. Amen.

The Second Joyful Mystery
The Visitation
Luke I, 39-50

At that time Mary got ready and hurried to a town in the hill country of Judea, where she entered Zachariah's home and greeted Elizabeth. When Elizabeth heard Mary's greeting, the baby leaped in her womb, and Elizabeth was filled with the Holy Spirit. In a loud voice she exclaimed, "Blessed are you among women, and blessed is the child you will bear! Blessed is she who has believed that the Lord would fulfil his promise to her!" And Mary said, "My soul glorifies the Lord, and my spirit rejoices in God my saviour for He has been mindful of the humble state of His servant. From now on all generations will call me blessed for the mighty One has done great thing for me, and holy is His name. His mercy extends to those who fear Him and holy is his name.

Prayers and Reflections

- Give us Lord, as you did Dolores, the desire to enter the homes and worlds of the lonely or fearful, to encourage, to offer hope and to strengthen with our attention the lives of your little ones. Amen.
- Give us Lord, as you did Dolores, a concern and engagement with pregnant women and great love for their children. Amen.
- Help us Lord, to pray with Dolores for those women who have undergone abortions and who need your mercy, love and forgiveness. Amen.
- Mother Mary, give to us, as you did to Dolores, a great love of others through small, hidden and seemingly insignificant acts of service and care. Show us through the humble acts of Dolores that great acts of change and devotion are brought as gifts to others. Amen.

Hail Mary, full of grace, the Lord is with thee. Blessed art thou among women and blessed is the fruit of thy womb, Jesus. Holy Mary, mother of God, pray for us sinners now and at the hour of our death. Amen.

The Third Joyful Mystery
The Nativity
Luke 2, 4-17

So Joseph also went up from Galilee, from the city of Nazareth, to Judea, to the city of David which is called Bethlehem. While they were there, the time came for the baby to be born and she gave birth to her firstborn, a son and wrapped him in swaddling cloths and placed him in a manger because there was no room available for them.

And there were shepherds living out in the fields nearby, keeping watch over their flocks at night. An Angel of the Lord appeared to them, and the glory of the Lord shone around them, and they were terrified. But the Angel said to them, "Do not be afraid, I bring you good news that will cause great joy for all the people. Today in the town of David a saviour has been born to you; he is the Messiah, the Lord. This will be a sign to you. You will find a baby wrapped in cloths and lying in a manger".

Suddenly a great company of the heavenly host appeared with the Angel, praising God and saying, "Glory to God in the highest and on Earth peace to those on whom His favour rests". When the Angels had left them and gone into Heaven the shepherds said to one another, "Let us go to Bethlehem and see this thing which has happened, which the Lord has told us about. So they hurried off and found Mary and Joseph, and the baby, who was lying in the manger.

Prayers and Reflections

- Help us Lord to pray with Dolores for all those struggling with the new circumstances of childbirth – strengthen us to offer our prayers and encouragement for those who suffer with post-natal depression or anxiety.
- Given us Lord, as you did Dolores, a special concern and affiliation with those who have adopted children and those who offer their lives as foster parents or the role of adoptive grandparents.
- Help us Lord, to speak lovingly as Dolores did to those suffering the loss of newborn babies or young children. Help us in our prayers and actions to embrace the truth of your redemptive suffering and our calling to share in the hurt and pain of others.

Hail Mary, full of grace, the Lord is with thee. Blessed art thou amongst women and blessed is the fruit of thy womb, Jesus. Holy Mary, Mother of God, pray for us sinners now and at the hour of our death. Amen.

The Presentation
Luke 2, 22-35

When the time came for the purification rites required by the Law of Moses, Joseph and Mary took him to Jerusalem to present him to the Lord. Now, there was a man in Jerusalem called Simeon who was righteous and devout. He was waiting for the consolation of Israel, and the Holy Spirit was on him. It had been revealed to him by the Holy Spirit that he would not die before he had seen the Lord's Messiah. Moved by the spirit, he went into the temple courts. When the parents brought in the child Jesus to do for him what the custom of the Law required, Simeon took him in his arms and praised God, saying:

> "Sovereign Lord, as you have promised, you may now dismiss your servant in peace, for my eyes have seen the salvation which you have prepared in the sight of all nations, a

light to reveal you to the gentiles, and the glory of your people Israel".

The child's father and mother marvelled at what was said about him. Then Simeon blessed them and said to Mary, his mother, "This child is destined to cause the falling and rising of many in Israel, and to be a sign that will be spoken against, so that the thoughts of many hearts will be revealed, and a sword will pierce your heart also".

Prayers and Reflections

- Help us Lord, as you did Dolores, to see the beauty and purpose of our Catholic traditions and culture. Strengthen us to support and encourage young parents to baptise their children and offer our practical support to sustaining baptismal promises in life.
- Give us Lord the courage to speak of the beauty, purpose and gifts of baptism to all those parents caught up in the immediate world and the concerns of the day.
- Give us Lord, the energy and desire to speak of heavenly things and of the coming of your Kingdom.

Hail Mary, full of grace, the Lord is with thee. Blessed art thou amongst women and blessed is the fruit of thy womb, Jesus. Holy Mary, Mother of God, pray for us sinners now and at the hour of our death. Amen.

The Finding of the Child Jesus in the Temple:
Luke 2, 41-52

Every year Jesus' parents went to Jerusalem for the festival of the Passover. When he was twelve years old, they went up to the festival, according to the custom. After the festival was over, while his parents were returning home, the boy Jesus stayed behind but they were unaware of it. Thinking he was in their company they travelled for a day. When they did not find him they went back to Jerusalem to find him. After three days they found him in the temple courts, sitting with the teachers, listening to them and asking them questions. Everyone was amazed at his understanding and his answers. When his parents found him, they were astonished and his mother said to him, "Son why have you treated us like this? Your father and I have been anxiously searching for you". "Why were you searching for me?" he asked, "Didn't you know I had to be in my father's house?" But they did not understand what he was saying to them. Then he went down to Nazareth with them and was obedient to them. But his mother treasured all these things in her heart.

Prayers and Reflections

- Make us attentive Lord, as Dolores was, to those parents who are afflicted with anxiety, fears or long-term concerns for their children.
- Help us, Mother Mary, to be understanding and available for parents who have courageously opened themselves to the gift of handicapped children and those who suffer long-term illness.
- Blessed Mary, we thank you for the particular gift of children with Downs Syndrome. We thank you for their joy, happiness and unique ability to bond families together through the love of your precious gift of life.
- Mother Mary, we pray for your Holy, Catholic and Apostolic Church. May she be a place where all parents and children may find support, rest and encouragement in their family life. May your church be a true family to all those who accept the

stress and difficulty of bringing children to mass.

Hail Mary, full of grace, the Lord is with thee. Blessed art thou amongst women and blessed is the fruit of thy womb, Jesus. Holy Mary, Mother of God, pray for us sinners now and at the hour of our death. Amen.

The Baptism of the Lord
Matthew 3, 1-2, 11-17

In those days John the Baptist came preaching in the wilderness of Judea and saying, "Repent, for the Kingdom of Heaven is at hand … I baptise you with water for repentance. But after me comes one who is more powerful than I, whose sandals I am not worthy to carry. He will baptise you with the Holy Spirit and with fire … Then Jesus came from Galilee to the Jordan to be baptised by John. But John tried to deter him, saying, "I need to be baptised by you, and do you come to me?"

Jesus replied, "Let it be so now, it is proper for us to do this to fulfil all righteousness". Then John consented.

As soon as Jesus was baptised, he went up out of the water. At that moment Heaven was opened, and he saw the spirit of God descending like a dove and alighting on him. And a voice from Heaven said, "This is my Son, whom I love, with him I am well pleased".

Prayers and Reflections

- Lead us Lord, as you did Dolores, into the fullness of new life, you commenced in our baptism. Help us to discover our true vocation of service and selfless obedience to your will.
- Mother Mary, you called and shaped Dolores in the way of attention to others – give us, as you gave her, a spirit of service and new life in the love of the lonely, the depressed and those whose hope is crushed.
- Mother Mary, you shaped Dolores in the service of others. Give us clarity in understanding your call to us to serve you and shape our priorities and love to others.

Hail Mary, full of grace, the Lord is with thee. Blessed art thou amongst women and blessed is the fruit of thy womb, Jesus. Holy Mary, Mother of God, pray for us sinners now and at the hour of our death. Amen.

The Wedding Feast at Cana
John 2: 1-11

On the third day, a wedding took place at Cana in Galilee. Jesus' mother was there, and Jesus and his disciples had also been invited to the wedding. When the wine was gone, Jesus' mother said to him, "They have no more wine". "Woman, why do you involve me? My hour has not come". His mother said to the servants, "Do whatever he tells you".

Nearby stood six stone water jars, the kind used by the Jews for ceremonial washing, each holding from twenty to thirty gallons. Jesus said to the servants, "Fill the jars with water", so they filled them to the brim. Then he told them, "Now draw some out and take it to the master of the banquet". They did so, and the master of the banquet tasted the water that had been turned into wine. He did not realise where it had come from, though the servants who had drawn the water knew.

Then he called the bridegroom aside and said, "Everyone brings out the choice wine first and then the cheaper wine after the guests have had too much to drink, but you have saved the best till now".

What Jesus did here in Cana of Galilee, was the first of the signs through which he revealed his glory; and his disciples believed in him.

Prayers and Reflections

- Blessed mother, we ask you to strengthen our desire to help others, as you strengthened the intentions of your servant Dolores. Give to us also the purpose and will to "do whatever he tells us", that we may come to love the service of Christ above self.
- Mother Mary, we ask you to intercede in our lives, through the prayers of the Rosary, as you did with your servant Dolores that we also may grow in peace, strength and knowledge of your son.
- Blessed mother, Dolores knew from her devotion to you, that you would always take care of her and never let her down. Give to us also this same knowledge and strength.

Hail Mary, full of grace, the Lord is with thee. Blessed art thou amongst women and blessed is the fruit of thy womb, Jesus. Holy Mary, Mother of God, pray for us sinners now and at the hour of our death. Amen.

The Proclamation of the Kingdom
Matthew 14.17, 23-25

From that time on, Jesus began to preach, "Repent for the Kingdom of Heaven has come near". Jesus went throughout Galilee, teaching in their synagogues, proclaiming the good news of the Kingdom and healing every disease and sickness among the people. News about him spread all over Syria, and people brought to him all who were ill with various diseases, those suffering severe pain, the demon possessed, those having seizures, and the paralysed, and he healed them. Large crowds from Galilee, the Decapolis, Jerusalem, Judea and the region across the Jordan followed him.

Prayers and Reflections

- Mother Mary, give to us your servants, the strength and confidence to cry the Gospel with our lives. As you blessed Dolores with this gift give us also the courage to proclaim the Gospel of Christ with our quiet, persistent and joyful service.
- Blessed mother, as your son healed the sick and the infirmities of many people, we ask for the blessing you gave Dolores, to see and understand those in pain or trouble, to bring comfort to those burdened and

- Blessed mother, lead us as you led Dolores, with humility for the broken hearted, for those unable to resist sin. Give to us, coupled with your servant Dolores, the ability to humble ourselves and pray with others "Thy will be done".
- Mother Mary, the Kingdom your son proclaimed is one of faith, service to others and love of neighbor. As you allowed Dolores to see your Kingdom in everyday events, give us also the ability to see the "Day of Salvation" in all our encounters and actions each day.

Hail Mary, full of grace, the Lord is with thee. Blessed art thou amongst women and blessed is the fruit of thy womb, Jesus. Holy Mary, Mother of God, pray for us sinners now and at the hour of our death. Amen.

The Transfiguration
Matthew 17, 1-9

After six days Jesus took with him Peter, James and John, the brother of James, and led them up a high mountain by themselves. There he was transfigured before them. His face shone like the sun and his clothes became as white as the light. Just then there appeared before them Moses and Elijah, talking with Jesus. Peter said to Jesus, "Lord, it is good for us to be here. If you wish I will put up three shelters – one for you, one for Moses and one for Elijah". While he was still speaking, a bright cloud covered them and a voice from the cloud said, "This is my Son, whom I love, with him I am well pleased. Listen to him!" When the disciples heard this, they fell face down on the ground, terrified. But Jesus came and touched them. "Get up", he said, "don't be afraid". When they looked up, they saw no one except Jesus. As they were coming down the mountain, Jesus instructed them, "Don't tell anyone what you have seen, until the Son of Man has been raised from the dead".

Prayers and Reflections

- Blessed Mary, the Transfiguration of your son Jesus is a foretaste of your glorious coming and fullness of our lives with you, as you always strengthened your servant Dolores, give us also faith in the truth of your resurrection.
- Mother Mary, as the Holy Spirit proclaimed the truth of your Son in the

transfiguration, "This is my beloved son, with whom I am well pleased, listen to him", may we also, coupled with your servant Dolores, glimpse the glory of your Son and may you grant peace to all who are entering suffering and death. Help us also to give comfort and strength to those who are anxious or troubled as you gave your calming peace to Dolores for all she encountered and in her final moments.

Hail Mary, full of grace, the Lord is with thee. Blessed art thou amongst women and blessed is the fruit of thy womb, Jesus. Holy Mary, Mother of God, pray for us sinners now and at the hour of our death. Amen.

The Institution of the Eucharist
Luke 22, 15-20

When the hour came, Jesus and his disciples reclined at table. And he said to them, "I have eagerly desired to eat this Passover with you before I suffer. For I tell you, I will not eat it again until it finds fulfilment in the Kingdom of God".

After taking the cup, he gave thanks and said, "Take this and divide it among you. And he took bread and broke it and gave it to them, saying "This is my body given for you, do this in memory of me".

Prayers and Reflections

- Blessed mother, in the institution of the Eucharist, your son gave himself totally for us. Help us, as you helped Dolores, to always be aware of the fullness of your son's life in the mass and in partnership with Dolores may we celebrate his life in gratefulness and humility.
- Blessed mother, the Eucharist means thanksgiving. As you gifted to Dolores a deep appreciation of all of life's gifts may we also take time to thank your son for the gift of life and the deep blessings of our community life in his Church.

Hail Mary, full of grace, the Lord is with thee. Blessed art thou amongst women and blessed is the fruit of thy womb, Jesus. Holy Mary, Mother of God, pray for us sinners now and at the hour of our death. Amen.

The Agony in the Garden
Luke 22, 39-46

Jesus went out as usual to the Mount of Olives and his disciples followed him. On reaching the place, he said to them, "Pray that you will not fall into temptation". He withdrew about a stone's throw beyond them, knelt down and prayed". "Father, if you are willing, take this cup from me, yet not my will but yours be done". An angel from Heaven appeared to him and strengthened him. And being in anguish, he prayed more earnestly, and his sweat was like drops of blood falling to the ground. When he rose from prayer and went back to his disciples, he found them asleep, exhausted from sorrow "Why are you sleeping?", he asked them, "Get up and pray so that you will not fall into temptation".

Prayers and Reflections

- Blessed mother, you called Dolores to experience long periods of suffering and illness. In our own trials, we pray that we also may overcome these difficulties with the patience and strength you gave Dolores.
- Mother Mary, you gave to Dolores the insight to accept her trials as redemptive

love and to know that her own struggles and pain partnered you in the redemptive love of your son for all people.
- Blessed Mary, we pray that, as you comforted Dolores in her long struggle with ill health, we may like her see the suffering of others and draw closer to them with the love of Christ in our hearts.
- Blessed mother of sorrows, you gave to your servant Dolores the humility to embrace your will in the midst of great suffering. Give us also the wisdom to humbly embrace your will in all things.
- Mother Mary, in the agony of Christ in the garden, the Holy Spirit sent an angel to comfort Jesus in his hour of need. We pray that you will graciously send to us your servant Dolores to comfort us and give us hope in our times of need.

Hail Mary, full of grace, the Lord is with thee. Blessed art thou amongst women and blessed is the fruit of thy womb, Jesus. Holy Mary, Mother of God, pray for us sinners now and at the hour of our death. Amen.

The Scouring at the Pillar
Mark 15, 9-15

"Do you want me to release to you the King of the Jews?" asked Pilate, knowing it was out of self-interest that the chief priests had handed Jesus over to him. But the chief priests stirred up the crowd to have Pilate release Barabbas instead. "What shall I do then with the one you call the King of the Jews?" Pilate asked them. "Crucify him", they shouted. "Why? What crime has he committed?" asked Pilate. But they shouted all the louder, "Crucify him!".

Wanting to satisfy the crowd, Pilate released Barabbas to them. He had Jesus flogged and handed him over to be crucified.

Prayers and Reflections

- Blessed mother, we know that your son suffered crucifixion because of his great love for us. We pray that you will show to us, as you did to your servant Dolores, that in imitating Christ, we will be called to suffer for others.
- Blessed Mary, as you called your servant Dolores to say yes to the needs of others, so may you call us to not only serve our families, children and loved ones, but all of those in whom we recognize need.

Hail Mary, full of grace, the Lord is with thee. Blessed art thou amongst women and blessed is the fruit of thy womb, Jesus. Holy Mary, Mother of God, pray for us sinners now and at the hour of our death. Amen.

The Crowning with Thorns
Matthew 27, 28-30, John 19, 46

And they stripped him and put a scarlet robe on him and, plaiting a crown of thorns, they put it on his head. And kneeling before him they mocked him, saying "Hail, King of the Jews!" and they spat on him, and took a reed and struck him on the head. Pilate went out again and said to them, "Behold I am bringing him out to you, so that you may know that I find no crime in him". So Jesus came out, wearing the crown of thorns and the purple robe. Pilate said to them, "Behold the man". When the chief priests saw him they said, "Crucify him, crucify him". Pilate said, "Take him yourselves for I find no crime in him".

Prayers and Reflections

- Blessed mother, when Pontius Pilate presents Jesus to his enemies with the

cry "ecce homo" (behold the man), he ultimately reveals the meaning of God's love for humanity. We pray, as your servant Dolores unequivocally identified herself with Christ in his sufferings, that we, like her, may claim our true humanity in service to others through Christ.
- Blessed Mary, mother of sorrows, we pray that, as you guided your servant Dolores to witness your love even at cost to herself, that we may do likewise.

Hail Mary, full of grace, the Lord is with thee. Blessed art thou amongst women and blessed is the fruit of thy womb, Jesus. Holy Mary, Mother of God, pray for us sinners now and at the hour of our death. Amen.

The Carrying of the Cross
(Via Dolorosa)

"As the soldiers led him away, they seized Simon from Cyrene, who was on his way in from the country, and they put the cross on him and made him carry it behind Jesus." (Luke 23. 36)

Prayers and Reflections

- Blessed mother Mary, in his suffering Jesus is surrounded by those who hate him and mock him, yet he endures this for us. Mother of Jesus, as you stood by your son in his sufferings so may we be aware of the presence of your servant Dolores in all that we see and do for and with your son.
- Blessed mother, the Via Dolorosa (the way of suffering) which your son calls all humanity to travel, is often filled with stumbling failure and despair. Give to us, as you gave to your servant Dolores, the strength of patience and persistence. Grant to us, as you granted to Dolores, the gift of eternal life.

Hail Mary, full of grace, the Lord is with thee. Blessed art thou amongst women and blessed is the fruit of thy womb, Jesus. Holy Mary, Mother of God, pray for us sinners now and at the hour of our death. Amen.

The Crucifixion
Luke 23, 35-47

The people stood watching and the rulers even sneered at him. They said, "He saved others; let him save himself if he is God's Messiah, the chosen one". The solders also came up and mocked him. They offered him wine vinegar and said, "If you are the King of the Jews, save yourself". There was a written note above him, which read: This is the King of the Jews.

One of the criminals who hung there hurled insults at him, "Aren't you the Messiah, save yourself and us!" But the other criminal rebuked him, "Don't you fear God", he said, "since you are under the same sentence? We are punished justly for what our deeds deserve. But this man has done nothing wrong". Then he said, "Jesus, remember me when you come into your Kingdom". Jesus answered him, "Truly I tell you, today you will be with me in paradise".

It was now about noon and darkness came over the whole land until three in the afternoon, for the sun stopped shining and the curtain of the temple was torn in two. Jesus called out with a loud voice, "Father, into your hands I commit my spirit". When he said this he breathed his last. The centurion, seeing what had happened, praised God and said, "Surely this was a righteous man". When all the people who had gathered to watch this sight saw what took place, they beat their breasts and went away. But all those who knew him, including the women who had followed him from Galilee, stood at a distance, watching these things.

Prayers and Reflections

- Blessed Mary, in the crucifixion of your son, he has fulfilled his great love for humanity, by laying down his life for each of us. In a similar way you called Dolores to lay down her life for others. Through her prayers and example may she highlight to us the great love she knew in Christ and lead us to the fullness of eternal life.
- Mother Mary, your servant Dolores knew that suffering for others is the great example of love for others. May she lead us to a deeper understanding of your cross as our ladder into Heaven.

Hail Mary, full of grace, the Lord is with thee. Blessed art thou amongst women and blessed is the fruit of thy womb, Jesus. Holy Mary, Mother of God, pray for us sinners now and at the hour of our death. Amen.

The Resurrection
Matthew 28, 1-10

Now, after the Sabbath, toward the dawn of the first day of the week, Mary Magdalen and the other Mary went to see the sepulchre. And behold, there was a great earthquake and an angel of the Lord descended from Heaven, rolled back the stone, and sat upon it. His appearance was like lightning, and his raiment white as snow. And for fear of him the guards trembled and became like dead men. But the Angel said to the woman, "Do not be afraid, for I know that you serve Jesus who was crucified. He is not here, for he has risen, as he said. Come; see the place where he lay. Then go quickly and tell his disciples that he has risen from the dead, and behold he is going before you to Galilee. There you will see him. Lo, I have told you". So they departed quickly from the tomb with fear and great joy, and ran to tell his disciples. And suddenly, Jesus met them and said, "Hail", and they came up and took hold of his feet and worshipped him. Then Jesus said to them, "Do not be afraid: go and tell my brothers to go to Galilee, and there they will see me".

Prayers and Reflections

- Mother Mary, in the resurrection of your Son, we see the fullness of eternal life coming to birth in us. We pray that with your servant Dolores we may catch a glimpse of this life and happily follow her steps into the fullness of Christ's Kingdom.
- Mother Mary, we know that your servant Dolores is with you and your son in Heaven, interceding and helping us. May we never be afraid to call upon her as a guide and example. We pray that through our ongoing relationship with your precious servant Dolores, we may be changed and completed in the resurrection of your son.

Hail Mary, full of grace, the Lord is with thee. Blessed art thou amongst women and blessed is the fruit of thy womb, Jesus. Holy Mary, Mother of God, pray for us sinners now and at the hour of our death. Amen.

The Ascension
Acts I, 6-11

So when they had come together, they asked him, "Lord will you at this time restore the Kingdom of Israel?" He said to them, "It is not for you to know times or seasons which the father has fixed by his own authority. But you shall receive power when the Holy Spirit has come upon you; and you shall be my witnesses in Jerusalem, and in all Judea and Samaria and to the end of the earth". And when he said this, as they were looking on, he was lifted up and a cloud took him out of their sight. And while they were gazing into Heaven as he went, two men stood by them in white robes, and said, "Men of Galilee, why do you stand looking into Heaven? This Jesus, who was taken up from you into Heaven, will come in the same way as you saw him go into Heaven".

Prayers and Reflections

- Mother Mary, St Paul teaches us to "set our minds on things that are above, not on things that are on earth". Blessed mother, in the life of your servant Dolores we see her great example of speaking up for those who suffer, of loving difficult people and of praying constantly for the needs of others. May we see in the selfless love of Dolores our clear path to redemption and eternal life.

- Blessed Mary, there are times in our lives when we cannot see your son clearly, when we are lonely or doubt his love. In the life of your servant Dolores we have an example of trust and love in the face of suffering and pain. May we also know that we can find and encounter your son in all our circumstances and that in the same manner you loved Dolores, you will also never let us down.

Hail Mary, full of grace, the Lord is with thee. Blessed art thou amongst women and blessed is the fruit of thy womb, Jesus. Holy Mary, Mother of God, pray for us sinners now and at the hour of our death. Amen.

The Descent of the Holy Spirit
Acts 2, 1-12

When the Day of Pentecost came, they were all together in one place. Suddenly, a sound like the blowing of a violent wind came from Heaven and filled the whole house where they were sitting. They saw what seemed to be tongues of fire that separated and came to rest on each of them. All of them were filled with the Holy Spirit and began to speak in other tongues as the spirit enabled them. Now there were staying in Jerusalem God-fearing Jews from every nation. When they heard the sound a crowd came together in bewilderment because each one heard their own language being spoken. Utterly amazed, they asked, "Aren't all these Galileans? How is it we hear them in our native language? We hear them declaring the wonders of God in our own tongues!" Amazed and perplexed, they asked one another "What does this mean?"

Prayers and Reflections

- Blessed mother, through the Holy Spirit we are restored to paradise, led into your Kingdom and adopted as your children. As you gave this grace to Dolores, may we also follow her example to be called children of light and share in the heavenly glory you have prepared for us.
- Mother Mary, the fruits of the Holy Spirit are love, joy, peace, patience, kindness, goodness, faithfulness, gentleness and self-control. As you gave these gifts to your servant Dolores, may we not be afraid

to ask her to lead us in the path of also fulfilling your call to live in the fullness of the spiritual gifts.

Hail Mary, full of grace, the Lord is with thee. Blessed art thou amongst women and blessed is the fruit of thy womb, Jesus. Holy Mary, Mother of God, pray for us sinners now and at the hour of our death. Amen.

The Assumption of Mary
Revelation 12, 1-6

A great sign appeared in Heaven: a woman clothed with the sun, with the moon under her feet and a crown of twelve stars on her head. She was pregnant and cried out in pain as she was about to give birth. Then another sign appeared in Heaven: an enormous red dragon with seven heads and ten horns and seven crowns on its heads. The dragon stood in front of the woman who was about to give birth, so that it might devour the child the moment he was born. She gave birth to a male child who "will rule all the nations with an iron sceptre". And her child was snatched up to God and to his throne. The woman went to a place prepared for her by God where she might be taken care of.

Prayers and Reflections

- Blessed mother, in Heaven you share in the glory of your son's resurrection and you anticipate the resurrection of all your sons and daughters. We pray that we may also see in the predestined life of Dolores an example of comfort, certain hope and powerful aid she offered to us. May we not be afraid to call upon her each day for her help and blessing.

- Blessed Mary, you are by your son's side in Heaven. May your prayers and the prayers of your servant Dolores be powerful in love and example and may they help us to Heaven.

Hail Mary, full of grace, the Lord is with thee. Blessed art thou amongst women and blessed is the fruit of thy womb, Jesus. Holy Mary, Mother of God, pray for us sinners now and at the hour of our death. Amen.

The Coronation of Mary
Psalm 45, 6-17

Your throne o God, will last forever and ever, a sceptre of Justice will be the sceptre of your Kingdom, you love righteousness and hate wickedness. Therefore your God has set you above your companions by anointing you with the oil of Joy. All your robes are fragrant with myrrh and aloes and cassia. All glorious is the princess within her chamber, her gown is interwoven with gold. In embroidered garments she is led to her King. I will perpetuate your memory through all generations, therefore the nations will praise you forever and ever.

Prayers and Reflections

- Mother Mary, we know that in Heaven you continue to offer your maternal love to those of us still on earth. As you called your servant Dolores to live life in the fullness of charity and self-sacrifice, may we also be intent on the things that are above, and through the prayers of Dolores may we know of your Son's love, forgiveness and unique calling to each of us.

    Pray for us Mother Mary

    Pray for us Dolores

    And may we hasten to meet our Lord in the fullness of life

Hail Mary, full of grace, the Lord is with thee. Blessed art thou amongst women and blessed is the fruit of thy womb, Jesus. Holy Mary, Mother of God, pray for us sinners now and at the hour of our death. Amen.

About the Author

Fr James Grant MAICD BA BTh GDip IS GDip Comp ST GDip Trauma Counselling. Born in Adelaide, and schooled in Essendon, Victoria. Fr James joined the Commonwealth Police in 1977 with an initial posting in Canberra. He has qualified as a martial arts instructor in Brazilian Jiu Jitsu, scuba diving and played first grade cricket for Northcote.

Fr James undertook theological studies at Melbourne University, graduating in 1984. Appointed to the UK as an associate priest, He became one of London's first white vicars to minister to the expanding West Indian community Fr James initiated his first interfaith gatherings in west London following the Brixton riots, after which he was appointed on short term placement to Berlin (west Germany) in 1988 and Budapest in 1989.

Fr James returned to Australia in 1989 where he was Senior Chaplain at Geelong Grammar School for seven years, followed by two years at St Michael's grammar and six years at The Peninsula School. He was noted for his pastoral care with a focus on martial arts, football and cricket as methods for building confidence in students.

In 2004 he was appointed a parish priest at St Stephens Richmond, then in 2005 Melbourne's first team vicar for the new parish of Jika Jika in Melbourne's north with responsibility for a large Sudanese refugee community. As Parish priest for the Preston area, he was a strong advocate for the Nuba people, of Sudan, who are experiencing genocide. He has built two schools in Northern India.

Fr James founded Chaplains Without Borders in 2004 to initiate new ventures into corporate and community organisations, and CWB grew to be Australia's largest chaplaincy service within 2 years. He went on to be appointed as the world's first chaplain to the casino industry in 2006 (Crown Enterprises Australia) a position he still retains.

As a leading traditionalist within the Australian church, Fr James supported the development to the Anglican Ordinariate in Australia and served on the national committee as secretary 2010-2011. Fr James was received into the Catholic Church and ordained as a Catholic Priest in September 2012 as a foundational priest for the Australian Ordinariate. In 2012 he was appointed National director for Ordinariate schools and to the Ordinariate governing council.

Fr James has continued to develop missions including Catholics in Business 2012 and Catholics in Mission and renewal in 2013. His CYA (Catholic Youth Academy) youth program works through Crown casino to develop confidence in de-motivated young Australians and find work placements within Crown. In 2013 he co-established the Renewal Centre.

He is the first Chaplain appointed to an A league soccer club in Australia at the largest Australian club, Melbourne Victory. He is involved with 9MM and 45ACP pistol competition and is completing PPL training for Helicopters

In 2015 Fr James established the Father James Grant foundation, implementing programs for de-motivated young Australians. The "mission Engage" program has now helped around 300 young Australians find their first Job. The Resurgence Group is a team designed to help parishes re-energize their community life.

    Web: www.chaplainswithoutborders.org
    www.catholicsinbusiness.org
    www.thefatherjamesgrantfoundation.org
    www.resurgence.org

www.ingramcontent.com/pod-product-compliance
Lightning Source LLC
Chambersburg PA
CBHW071427160426
43195CB00013B/1837